D1356851

Quiltmaking
in patchwork & appliqué

Michele Walker

EBURY
PRESS
LONDON

For James

Published by Ebury Press
National Magazine House
72 Broadwick Street
London W1V 2BP

First impression 1985

Copyright © 1985 by Frances Lincoln Limited
Text copyright © 1985 by Michele Walker

Quiltmaking in Patchwork and Appliqué was
conceived, edited and produced by Frances Lincoln Ltd,
Apollo Works, 5 Charlton Kings Road, London NW5 2SB.

ISBN 0 85223 433 3

Filmset by Vantage Photosetting Ltd., London and Eastleigh

Printed and bound in Italy

CONTENTS

INTRODUCTION

None of the contemporary artists whose works are to be found in this book started out with the intention of becoming a quilt-maker. A quilt, after all, is simply a warm bedcover with a padded interlining, and the discovery that within this prosaic-sounding medium lies an art form rich in visual and tactile expression can, more often than not, happen almost by accident.

My own discovery of quiltmaking came during a period spent in Canada: I visited several quilt exhibitions and, inspired by these, embarked on the making of a full-scale quilt. Rather like the early American quilt-makers, my living conditions were cramped and my resources, as well as my expertise, limited. This particular quilt, and several that followed, were made to traditional patterns and from them I was to acquire a great deal of technical know-how. As a result, I began to build up an understanding of the relationship between the design and the construction of the quilt, and to appreciate the endlessly varied possibilities that are offered by the craft.

On my return to England, I met Joen Zinni Lask. The meeting coincided with her exhibition of Amish quilts, and this was later followed by a travelling exhibition of American pieced quilts which was arranged by Jonathan Holstein. I found these quilts tremendously exciting and they gave me a continuing source of inspiration. I was particularly drawn to the Amish use of colour on dark grounds and to the more general American techniques of using repeated blocks to create large geometric patterns.

Maybe as a result of my training as a graphic designer, these abstract patchwork patterns were more appealing to me than the naturalistic and pictorial images that are so often created with appliqué, and this individual preference is reflected throughout this book.

By this time I had begun to meet both quiltmakers and collectors who shared my enthusiasm for quilts. In 1979, we formed the Quilters' Guild as a forum for quiltmakers to meet, exchange ideas and information and hold exhibitions. This is now a national organization, and the interest in quiltmaking has never been stronger.

Those who want to learn about quiltmaking will generally start by copying traditional patterns, but after a while most people begin to look beyond these confines, and want to create something more individual. Such a development is necessary if the craft is to be kept alive, although it can be difficult to break away from tradition, and the process is usually a gradual one.

In this book, I have suggested some new approaches, but these still relate to the

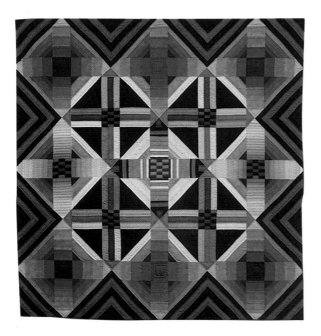

LEFT *'Interfacings 1'. American. 1983.*
183 × 183cm (72 × 72in). Nancy Crow.

OPPOSITE *'Cubic Log Cabin'. English. 1982.*
173 × 164cm (68 × 65in). Pauline Burbidge.

traditional practice of using a grid and/or repeated block as the basis of the design.

To give a wider design horizon than my own views, I have included the work of several contemporary makers and asked them to explain their ideas and sources of inspiration so that their achievements can be shared. Although they have all departed from tradition and their quilts are truly innovative, these quiltmakers all acknowledge their debt to the past.

Those who are quiltmaking today find themselves in a very different environment. Quilts are no longer a necessity as bedcovers, and quiltmaking is often now regarded as a modern artistic medium rather than simply a sentimental link with the past. Most of the works commissioned by galleries and other public and private collectors from leading quiltmakers are often destined to be hung rather than used as bedcovers. The makers choose to work with fabric and colour because they enjoy exploring a medium which is tactile as well as visual.

Links are now developing between contemporary designers here and in the United States. Both countries have benefited in the past from the interchange of ideas and I am very pleased to be able to further this in this book. I feel the same excitement when I see the work of American artists such as Michael James, Jan Myers, Linda MacDonald and Nancy Crow as I did when I first saw traditional American block patterns.

How to use this book

I have divided the book into four main chapters. The first is a gallery of quilts, traditional and contemporary, specially chosen for their visual content. The idea is to demonstrate the enormous breadth and range of artistic possibilities offered by the medium, and to provide sources of inspiration and starting points for new designs.

The quilts are divided into several broad categories. These can be looked at in conjunction with the design chapter which follows. The aim here is to discuss various design theories that should help those who want to move on from copying old patterns to creating more innovative designs. There is an analysis of common types of design, and

several sections have been illustrated deliberately with black and white, rather than colour, drawings to make the underlying principles of tone, grid, shape and perspective easier to grasp. The chapter ends with a discussion of different approaches to design using the work of five contemporary quiltmakers as examples.

The last two chapters, on sewing and quilting, describe all the skills and techniques necessary to make a quilt, including the choice of suitable fabrics and the making of templates. All the techniques are clearly illustrated with step-by-step drawings. Although many of the fabrics illustrated are patterned, this is simply to make the diagrams clearer, and should not be taken as an indication that patterned fabrics are more suitable for patchwork than plain ones.

The sewing and quilting techniques described are the result of my own experiences as a teacher. The emphasis is on good workmanship, as design and technical skill are inextricably bound together. Crooked patches and uneven edges in a hundred-year-old quilt are admired as an endearing quirk but they are rarely acceptable in contemporary work. Some techniques have been deliberately left out, as I find that they tend to take precedence over the actual design.

At the end of the book I have included a short section on caring for quilts. The emphasis here is on general care: very valuable antique quilts should receive the same specialist treatment that would be given to a good painting. A selection of block patterns and of template shapes completes the book.

The aim throughout this book is to emphasize the design element in quiltmaking. The construction of a quilt is enjoyable in itself and most people start by making up traditional patterns, but it is infinitely more stimulating and pleasurable to make up a quilt from your own design.

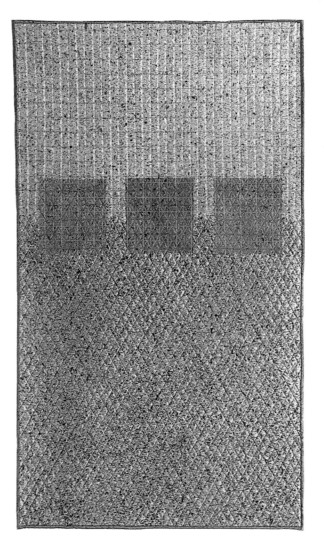

'Three Squares'. English. 1982.
50 × 84cm (20 × 33in). Diana Harris.

'Metamorphosis'. American. 1983.
213 × 213cm (84 × 84in). Michael James.

Quilts from the collection of Jane Kasmin.

1. QUILT GALLERY

All the quilts in this section have been chosen for their visual
qualities. Some are traditional in the finest sense, representing a
popular view of what a quilt should look like. Others, both
antique and modern, break all the rules of conventional
quiltmaking but in so doing reach another visual level and
transcend the simple materials from which they were made.
Some quilts were obviously made principally for show and are
highly decorative, while others convey a much deeper purpose
and meaning in their design and seem to awaken more primitive
responses.

The quilts have been divided into three main categories: one-
patch patterns, repeated blocks and single image designs, which
do not necessarily depend on a repeated unit. Within these
groupings, the quilts have been arranged from the viewpoint of
design rather than that of chronology or pattern. The aim is to
invite the reader to compare the old with the new, to consider
why certain colour formations and contrasts work, why some
departures from the conventional norms are so effective, and
why some designs are vibrant and exciting while others are
simply pretty. The selection is inevitably and unashamedly a
personal one and some popular patterns have deliberately been
left out to make room for others that I find more innovative and
original.

In the last century, quiltmaking was often considered a daily
chore but also gave an opportunity for recreation and creativity.
By no means all the traditional quilts were masterpieces: some
were hastily thrown together and used until they had worn to
shreds; others were overdecorated monstrosities made by
women who had more time than design sense. Those quilts that
have been treasured and passed down through the generations
usually had something special to offer in the way of design. The
maker has explored the potential of colour, for example, or the
three-dimensional possibilities of the medium.

The amount of time and effort that went into making a good
quilt should not be underestimated. Contemporary makers draw
inspiration from such works but use them as a challenge. The
traditional quilt no longer only evokes a nostalgic feeling for the
past: it is seen as a unique art form and a departure point for new
and exciting directions in quiltmaking which will take it firmly
into the future.

ONE-PATCH DESIGNS

One-patch patterns are those in which the design is built up by repeating one single fabric shape throughout, depending solely on changes in tone and colour and, perhaps, on quilting (as in Deirdre Amsden's 'Colour Washes') to activate the surface. Within these confines, however, is an area rich in interpretation. The range of quilts in this section forms two distinct categories from the point of view both of design style and also of sewing technique.

The quilts in the first group, produced mainly by American makers during the last century, combine economy of effort with a strong visual statement. The designs are bold and simple, sophisticated and surprisingly modern in feeling, considering that they were made some time ago. The shapes are simple – squares and triangles sewn together with a small running stitch – and the quiltmakers, who were fully aware of the application of tone and colour, used them to explore the illusion of space.

In the second group are the mosaic pattern quilts created from repeated hexagons, small triangles or diamonds. Mosaic-type quilts were labour-intensive, elaborate and decorative, and are associated with traditional English patchwork. They were often made by ladies of leisure who probably also embroidered, for most quilts of this type show excellent workmanship although the designs are occasionally rather confused. The best quilts, however, are almost kaleidoscopic, with something of the quality of marquetry – a complete contrast to the bold and simple statements of the utility quilters.

Although the two groups have been deliberately intermingled in this chapter, they are easily distinguishable.

◆ Painted Rectangles ◆

At the far end of the scale from the intricately pieced mosaic, good basic patchwork can be like painting with fabric. Country traditions sometimes make folk art of patchwork: the intuitive placing of colours and shapes in this simplest of quilts gives it a painterly quality.

Welsh country quilts were generally less intricate than those made in other regional traditions, for instance, in the North of England. This particular quilt displays several Welsh characteristics: the use of simple rectangular patches, the 'snail-creep' spirals of quilting that pucker the surface, and the combination of strong, bold colours.

Painterly colours

The receptiveness of the local wool to various dyes made many brilliant, soft and subtle tones available to the quiltmaker. The earthy richness and the solidity of the colour is reminiscent of the texture of oil paints mixed on a palette.

This country quilt was undoubtedly put together for everyday use: a utility quilt. The thick fabrics with their warm filling must have been laborious to quilt, using the strongest cotton or linen thread, and working in stab stitch, since such thick material would have made running stitch practically impossible.

People who look to patchwork for its cotton-frock nostalgia, for intricate geometrical puzzles or for the secure rhythms of repeating block patterns may well wonder what I see in this raw, unsophisticated quilt. But look at it as an exercise in colour, and you will perhaps find in it the visual depth that is so characteristic of primitive art. There is even something here that recalls a Paul Klee painting. The design element is intuitive, almost artless: the maker of this quilt had a natural feeling for colour and form, which has made a painting from these scraps of coloured wool.

An assemblage of shapes

The patches, although apparently put together as haphazardly as a group of colour swatches, have an instinctive balance of colour and shape that is pleasing. The whole is satisfying in its scale and proportions. The centre consists of a panel of smaller rectangular bricks, where colour seems secondary to texture.

Around this central core are two rows of rectangles, on a larger scale and in a different mode. Here, colour is the important element, though still muted. Finally, large slabs – almost strips – of red and black make a decisive and dramatic border. They contain the motley collection of pieces in their frame, but are firmly linked by their relationship to the central red patch, which is the focus of the whole composition.

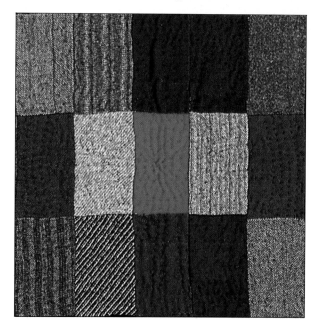

Detail of the centre of the quilt shows the beginning of the snail-creep spiral of quilting stitches, a common feature of Welsh quilts.

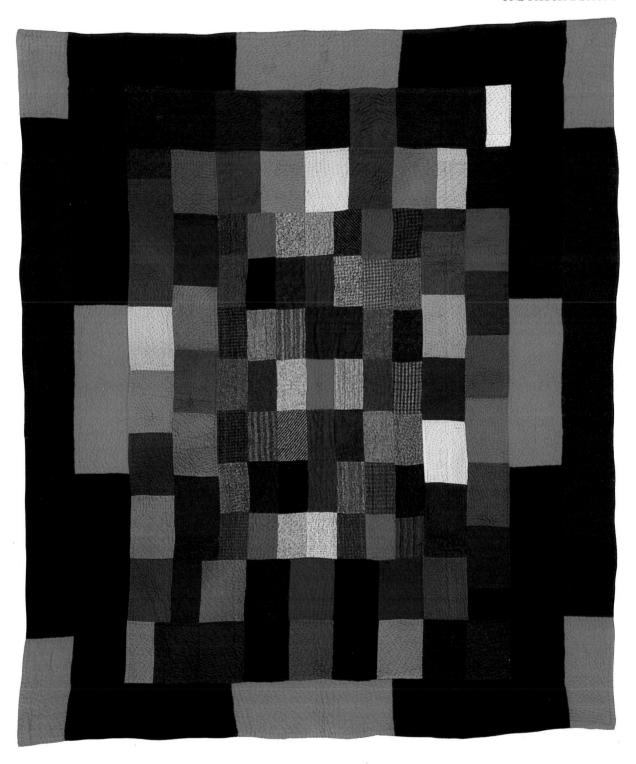

Hand stitched wools and tweeds, filled with wool and hand quilted.
Welsh. Late 19th century. 202 × 178cm (80 × 70in).

✦ Trip Around the World ✦

A spectrum of colours combines to form a powerful image: a vibrant diamond shape expanding within a deep framing border. The interchange of light and dark colours in the centre suggests a lit stage, dramatic and compelling. The extreme contrast between the deep blue-black of night and the bright sunny yellow is a reminder of the pattern's alternative name, Sunshine and Shadow. The colours seem to allude to the warmth of the sun and the earth, contrasting with both the cold depths of the sea and the lightness and luminosity of the clear sky.

Such is the boldness of the image and the complexity of the colour relationships that the design seems to transcend the simplicity of the basic structure: a grid of plain squares within well-proportioned borders. A mosaic of simple square shapes represents economy of resources: the adventure and extravagance is in the deployment of colour.

Economy has always typified the classic American utility quilt, often lending the designs a strength and graphic directness that accounts for their appeal to today's tastes. One of the strongest quiltmaking traditions was developed by the Amish, and it is interesting to trace part of its evolution in this particular quilt.

The Amish in the Midwest

The Amish were a Swiss-German Protestant sect. The earliest immigrants settled in Pennsylvania in the early 18th century, and it is among their descendants that Amish quiltmaking traditions perhaps remained purest. Most Amish quilts were made of straight, simple piecing, often having bold geometrical motifs such as the diamond in a square (see pp 86–7).

A century after the original immigration, groups split away and moved westwards towards Indiana and Ohio. It is probably in these latter communities that the quilt seen

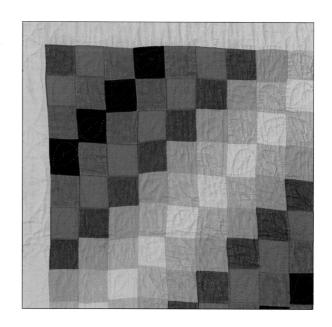

here was made. Amish quiltmakers in Ohio seem to have been influenced by other styles of quiltmaking, without losing their distinctive identity. The Trip Around the World pattern, with its small units comparable in size to the patches in many repeating blocks, was far more popular here than the geometric designs based on large pieces of fabric. The overall quilt tended to be rectangular rather than the square shape customary in Pennsylvania.

And it was in Ohio that there was perhaps the greatest development in the use of colour. In some ways the abandoning of the characteristic strong, rich, home-dyed fabric colours is regrettable, yet with an unerring colour sense, the Amish harnessed the products of new dyeing technology to their design vision. The somewhat acidic pastel tints that became available around the turn of the century are essentially harsh, but here they attain a vigorous balance.

Each of the square patches is quilted with the outline of a simple leaf. The yellow framing band has a more flowing pattern of linking ovals and diamonds.

Hand sewn cotton. Cotton filling. Hand quilted.
American/Ohio Amish. c 1900. 229 × 203cm (90 × 80in).

◆ Framed Hexagons ◆

Regular hexagons set together make the honeycomb pattern that fascinated the makers of Middle Eastern mosaics, and became one of the earliest institutionalized patchwork patterns. Its attractiveness was extolled in women's magazines of the 1830s, and to many amateur quiltmakers in Britain the hexagon is still almost synonymous with patchwork.

The regular hexagon has six equal sides. It breaks down into six equilateral triangles (the divisions of isometric or triangular graph paper, on which it is easy to see the relationship between the hexagon and the wide diamond of the six-pointed stars and Tumbling Blocks). However, the simple all-over honeycomb of regular hexagons is the most familiar: the six-sided figures fit together as snugly as a grid of squares. Accuracy is very important here, because cumulative error is more difficult to eliminate when working with fabric in this more complicated shape: hence the need for carefully cut templates and backing papers.

It is characteristic of the hexagon grid to seem 'pretty' and decorative, rather lacking

the boldness of the utility quilts. It is easy for the shape and identity of the individual patch to be submerged by the fabric print, or, as a multi-patch rosette motif, to be joined indiscriminately in all-over patterning. Indeed, it is sad to see so many hexagon quilts, both old and more recent, with so little overall impact that the eye retires in confusion – perhaps to seek some solace investigating the tantalizing scraps of information that the torn-up letters used for backing papers sometimes reveal.

The sense of structure

The quilt on these pages shows a highly pleasing use of hexagons to create a strong overall image. A structure of white patches 'keys' the multicoloured randomness into a focal area at the centre and a series of borders. Individual white rosettes repeat to highlight the design at regular intervals. White is a stark contrast, but its harsh effect is softened by the small scale of the patches, by their generally decorative shape, and by the fact that so many of the coloured prints have white as the ground colour.

The grandeur of the design is enhanced by two elaborate printed border strips, the richness and complexity of which go well with the colourful mood of the mosaic.

Here is a patchwork quilt in the strongest tradition, using a treasure trove of fabrics collected over a long period of time: a true scrap-bag quilt, made of dress cottons probably accumulated in a middle-class household. It would be a vast task to identify and date so many different fabrics; some patterns were produced from about 1825 onwards, while others date from around the middle of the century.

A variety of patterns in multicoloured fabrics seen in close-up give the patches a busy feel, which needs the white areas for relief. Only at some distance do the elements blend into an overall surface that is alive and interesting.

Hand stitched coverlet. Cotton chintz hexagonal patches.
English. c 1850. 259 × 236cm (102 × 93in).

◆ Church Window Rosettes ◆

The 'long' hexagon is sometimes called Church Window. Joined together into rosettes, as in this quilt, the elongated shape is clearly seen. Perhaps the slight vertical emphasis gives the pattern some lightness, as opposed to the more predictable symmetry of regular hexagons.

The lightness is partly due, of course, to the network of plain white patches, an outline grid keeping each rosette distinct and in its place. This quilt has no focusing device, no borders framing a formal unity of design – but these white patches are an essential, understated structural element, that saves the mass of different patches from total confusion.

An exercise in nostalgia

In its fabrics and colours as well as in its lack of design, this quilt seems less sophisticated than the Framed Hexagon quilt on the previous page. It has a softer farmhouse rather than town house feel. Perhaps because the fabrics are evocative of little girls' and housemaids' dresses, we feel drawn in to the painstaking processes of making all these tiny patches and sewing them all together. They awaken our sympathy and curiosity about the lives and fates of the wearers.

People still hoard favourite fabrics and relish the challenge that honeycomb patchwork entails. It would be best to enjoy and appreciate quilts of this sort as artefacts from the past, and not merely to copy them in a world that has moved on. Quiltmaking with hexagons offers other challenges as Susan Carr's quilt on pp28–9 demonstrates.

Today's fabric prints, even the reproductions of the ones we see here, use different fibres and dyestuffs, and need more careful handling to mix and blend so subtly. Colours tend to be brighter and harsher now, and you can no longer jumble them together and let simple harmony result.

Fabric patterns can emphasize or disguise the shape of the basic patch. Fine dense patterning acts like tone, filling outlines and joining adjacent patches as if seamlessly. In the top detail the colours in the fabric pattern disrupt the hexagon shape; in the lower picture, the shapes of the concentric rosettes are clear.

Hand stitched cotton dress prints, lightly filled with cotton and hand quilted.
English. Late 19th century. 213 × 197cm (84 × 77in).

◆ Sunshine and Shadow ◆

This functional, unpretentious workaday Mennonite quilt is the epitome of a simple, well-ordered life: sunshine and shadow reflecting the harmony of a rural existence, where sunrise and sunset form the basis of the simple rhythm of a country routine.

The Mennonites as quiltmakers

Like the Amish, the Mennonites are a Protestant sect who settled in Pennsylvania in the 17th century. Strongly pacifist and highly philanthropic, most became craftsmen and farmers in self-sufficient communities. To this day they maintain a Christian way of life that allows the modern world to encroach on it as little as possible.

Mennonites usually made their quilts in dark and sober colours, with small touches of a brilliant contrast. Fabrics were often woollen flannels and suitings. Light greys and coffee tones are characteristic colours.

While the stricter Amish denied themselves the use of any patterned fabrics, the Mennonites might use subtle, discreet all-over patterns. Here some patches are slightly mottled with fine stripes or tweedy flecks, relieving the flatness of the rather drab colours and making the fabrics even more reminiscent of landscape textures, of the subtle graining of sand, gravel and earth. The colours and pattern are an abstraction of familiar landscape. They are also reminiscent of the parched desert colours used by the Hopi and other Indians in their textiles.

The basic square

The simplest of one-patch shapes, squares build sophisticated patterns through their deployment of colour. Set on their points to become diamonds, squares instantly create a tension across a surface. Here colours are distributed concentrically, to reinforce the square shape of the overall quilt, but the rows of diamonds have an expanding, radiating effect, and the combination of gradated tones with abrupt contrasts keeps the surface optically alive.

The beiges and greys, warm and cool neutrals suggesting sunshine and shade, tend to merge into one another unless a distinct light-dark contrast marks their division. Their slow gradations of tone suggest depth, with black receding so far as almost to sink into the surface. Against these neighbours the capacity for warm red to come forward is exaggerated, and the red patches seem at times to move on a plane in front of the other colours.

The fabric pieces would have been graded and laid out according to colour, and the rows pieced diagonally, so that the quiltmaker would have seamed squares rather than diamonds. This straightforward utilitarian product is much in tune with the philosophy of its makers.

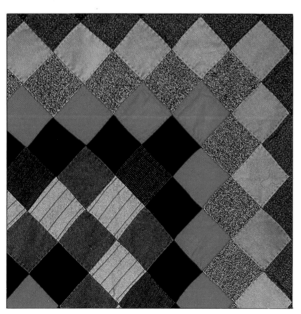

This close-up shows the texture of the different fabrics and the quilting stitches that outline each square: a feature of American quiltmaking, and typically Mennonite in its simplicity.

Hand stitched woollen suitings and flannels. Wool filling. Squares outline quilted.
American. Late 19th century. 200 × 200cm (79 × 79in).

◆ Victorian Mosaic ◆

The Victorian penchant for mosaics did not always produce quilts with a predominant overall design rather than a mere confusion of patterning. In this quilt, however, the sampler-like display of different patchwork patterns is organized into a compelling structure, a framework with contrasts of scale and depth, with a strong central image and delightful detailing.

A display of wealth and skill

Such quilts were often made by middle-class women with time on their hands and a wealth of opulent silk, satin and velvet dress materials to choose from. They might raid their own scrap-bags, or perhaps glean off-cuts from their dressmakers. These ladies of leisure spent much time on the piecing of elaborate and intricate designs, using minute templates and thousands of patches – not all to such disciplined and satisfying final results. The quilt was a display of their artistic skills, the opulence of the fabrics signalling status, taste and refinement.

The structure: frame within frames

The different panels within the quilt continue to delight the senses, the light-reflecting surface of the fabrics suggesting facets of mother-of-pearl here, marquetry there, and occasionally evoking the scintillating background infill with which Gustav Klimt textured many of his most powerful paintings.

In the centre are clusters of six-pointed stars linked with hexagons. The stars are gradually submerged into the Tumbling Block pattern, one point of a star forming a third of a Tumbling Block.

This central pattern is framed by a border of four rows of Tumbling Blocks with large diamonds in each corner square, making a ribbon-like zig-zag pattern with the consistent use of black as one of the three diamonds. The Tumbling Blocks border is

itself framed with a new triangular border, where the scale and grid changes from isometric to squares, making triangles from half-squares. In each corner, Tumbling Blocks again appear, but this time in a much smaller form.

A new Tumbling Block border is edged at the top and bottom by a repeat of the larger triangles. And, finally, the outer border follows the large triangular pattern at the sides, while at the top and bottom the triangles are set with parallelograms.

The Tumbling Block pattern does not seem to have been widely used before the 1850s, and this quilt is almost identical to one which is signed and dated 'August 31st 1877', so it seems safe to date it around 1880.

The vast array of different colours and patterns are kept in tune by a disciplined structure, but they share an underlying harmony in their common luminous texture. They combine in a rich abstract picture.

Detail from the right edge of the quilt shows the textural richness and subtle patterning of the silks and brocades, and hints at the extraordinarily broad range of fabrics.

Hand stitched silks. Tumbling Blocks, stars and other template shapes.
Coverlet. English. c 1880. 218 × 188cm (86 × 74in).

◆First and Last & Welsh Bricks◆

In patchwork, as in so many other forms of design, simplicity often produces the maximum visual impact. These two utility quilts, made from plain, everyday fabrics, are an excellent example of this. Their beauty lies in the good use of limited materials and a restrained design and in their subtle, uneven variation in tone and texture. The constraints imposed by the strictly utilitarian function of such quilts have happy, if accidental, design effects. The shapes are simple, and so the clear, bold lines of the design can make the maximum impact, without the distraction of an elaborate border, and the limited range of colours allows the patchwork pattern to develop fully, without the counteracting effect produced by highly patterned fabrics.

First and Last

Iona Heath, the maker of this quilt, has always been drawn to the patchwork tradition of reworking an old idea to find something new and alive and has made many quilts for her family to use and enjoy.

Some years ago she was given some bundles of suiting samples and, following a quiltmaking tradition, has used these same ingredients as a constant source of new designs, mixing doctor's red flannel with greys to provide an interesting contrast. Her commitment to exploring what can be done with the combination of red, grey and black gives her designs something in common with the 19th-century military quilts that were made out of old uniforms.

The design for 'First and Last' was taken from a quilt seen in a photograph in Walter Evans' book of the same name, but by the time Iona Heath had finished her quilt it was clear that she had used the block in a quite different way from the original; a perfect illustration of the effect that the personality of each maker has on a design.

The basic shape is a rectangle made by two triangles and a parallelogram. The chevron-type pattern is based on a repeated unit but has a strong overall mosaic effect. The work is machine stitched.

Welsh Bricks

An American influence can be detected in this Welsh brick pattern quilt from the manner in which the bricks are laid – in a diagonal fashion rather than horizontally and vertically – producing a tauter and more dynamic result. The quilting pattern, however, is very similar to one commonly used in Glamorgan. The bricks themselves are arranged in a simple way, staggered like real bricks. The colour in the quilt is distributed well and the materials are hard-wearing and sensible – cotton twills once used for workshirts and maids' dresses.

Welsh Bricks. Hand stitched and quilted cotton. Welsh. 1900–20. 106 × 106cm (42 × 42in).

*'First and Last'. Machine stitched tailor's samples. Filled with a blanket.
English. 1983. 230 × 220cm (90 × 86in). Iona Heath.*

◆ Summer Garden ◆

Susan Carr likes to use traditional patterns in a way that conveys highly contemporary visions. Her favourite shapes are the wide diamond, the hexagon and the triangle, all of which are derived from isometric graph paper, and her designs include glimpses of the conventional patterns such as stars and rosettes which these shapes are generally used to make. But starting from this point, her quilts go on to show some of the visually exciting ways in which these traditional shapes can be used to experiment with colour and pattern.

Like many other modern quilt artists, Susan Carr uses plain fabrics to give the outlines their maximum impact, and she chooses slightly muted, home-dyed colours, giving her a palette of soft greens, blues, pinks and ochres. These are used to create a movement of light and tone across the surface of the quilt in a way which is becoming a hallmark of her work.

Design development

Most of Susan Carr's quilts start with pure pattern, any figurative qualities emerging almost by accident. The shapes and colours create a fragmented design in which one basic shape and pattern is gradually taken over by another. This quilt began with a series of pattern experiments using the triangular grid on which wide diamonds and hexagons are drawn. In the early stages of the design, the light and dark greens were used as a background, with the yellow and pink stars interacting over them. The pattern seemed to suggest the colours of a suburban garden in summer, so the patches were then more consciously manipulated to create this impression more strongly. Susan Carr pushed the pattern further until she was satisfied with it in terms of pure design as well as for its almost pictorial quality. Two blues and a brown were added for interest and to give the

effect of shadows and – bearing in mind that blue is a receding colour – distance at the top of the quilt. This gradual progression from greens and yellows through to blues and brown is based on an organized system, the colours being grouped into sets of three which change places alternately to create a gradual colour shift over the work.

Another colour sequence, this time working horizontally, slowly transmutes the dark blue or green stars at the edges into orange and yellow. The separate pieces fragment into various configurations, emphasizing the different component shapes: triangles, hexagons and diamonds.

Patterns formed with hexagons and wide diamonds are traditionally made up with backing papers, but this would take time that Susan Carr would prefer to spend on design. She therefore organizes her work so that the pieces can be sewn together into strips by machine.

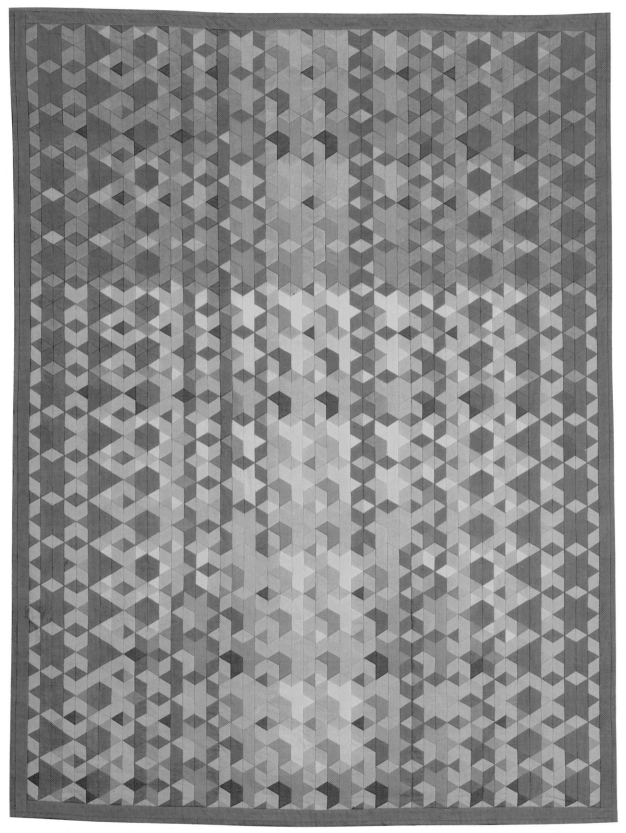

Machine stitched and hand-dyed cotton fabrics. English. 1984. 168 × 130cm (66 × 51in). Susan Carr.

✦ Lone Star & Harvest Star ✦

Star quilts are among the most spectacular, both in their visual impact and in their stitching expertise. The diamond-shaped patches, with their two bias edges, are tricky and need experienced handling.

Both these quilts are functional and everyday. The patterns were popular all over America, changing their name according to where they were made. Inland, they might have some agricultural connotation, and by the coast a more maritime theme.

Lone Star

This design is also known as Star of Bethlehem or Star of the East. A single dynamic shape is blazoned across a deep black surface. Such star designs were common among the Mennonites in both Pennsylvania and Canada at the end of the 19th century. As well as the statutory plain fabrics, a few pale blues have barely discernible stripes or paisley patterning.

The maker of this heavy quilt has thriftily used any odd pieces of black fabric for the background, though they are unified by the curving quilting lines running across the whole surface.

The skilful maker, however, reserved her most devoted attention for piecing the star. The vivid colours glow against their black ground and, within the points of the star, the subtle manipulation of tonal contrasts makes the surface vibrant, so that the image radiates, as stars should. The quiltmaker knew just what she was doing in placing the most brilliant colour – the single yellow diamond marking each tip of the star echoes the glow at the centre.

The whole quilt lies beautifully flat, a fine achievement in bulky woollen fabrics.

Harvest Star

This popular design has many names, including Prairie Star, Harvest Sun, Touching Star and Colonial Star; in Massachusetts it is called Ship's Wheel. Sometimes a double sawtooth border is added, as can be seen in the example here.

Compared with the Lone Star, the white background reduces the brilliance of the colours, producing a more muted, gentler effect. Red, yellow and green balance evenly in their intensity, and are distributed regularly in circles throughout the stars, with a result that is more like a colour exercise than just a visually pleasing pattern. However, this is a fine old everyday quilt in the best tradition. This particular colour combination is typically Pennsylvania German. Colours used in quilts, as in flags, help to identify their origins.

Harvest Star. Hand stitched cottons. Cotton filling. Hand quilted in diamond grid. Pennsylvania German. c 1880. 234 × 234cm (92 × 92in).

Lone Star. Hand stitched wools. Wool filling. Hand quilted in radial pattern.
Canadian Mennonite. c 1885. 190 × 178cm (75 × 70in).

◆ Strippy with Squares ◆

It was in quilting rather than in patchwork that the women of the north-east of England displayed their needlework skills. The strippy is the local specialization, deriving, perhaps from economies in the use of both fabric and time. Strippies are usually in two contrasting colours. Red and white was always a favourite combination, ever since the 1830s when Turkey red became available as the first permanent red dye. (In frugal households the white fabric probably derived from unpicked flour sacks.) Later, when the fabric was bought specially, the strippy remained an indigenous style.

Materials were always simple cottons or cotton sateens, to show off the quilting. The stripes might be on both sides, or the backing might be plain. Stripes were about 20cm (8in) across, and usually ran from the top to the bottom of the quilt; the quilting patterns followed the path of the strips.

The continuance of the strippy tradition was perhaps partly due to the convenience of the making process. Many of the quilting patterns are linear; the outline was marked on each panel, one at a time, when the quilt was already set up in the frame. This saved the laborious premarking necessary on quilts where an image is centred.

Northerners set great store by orderliness and keeping up appearances. In their gardens and allotments, the rows of vegetables ran parallel and weedless and they believed in hard work – virtues echoed in the design of their quilts. It is a well-known misconception that the sheer amount of effort that goes into the making of something in itself brings merit, but the fine workmanship of the strippy demonstrates the good side of this equation, where the simplest materials are dignified by sheer craftsmanship into beautiful artefacts.

The dotty side

The other side of this quilt, opposite, is one of quiltmaking's mysteries. Red patches (10cm or 4in square) have been applied to the backing fabric before the whole was quilted. This whim is without precedent. Perhaps just this amount of fabric was left over (and nothing useful could ever be allowed to go to waste); perhaps there were too few pieces to make a pattern. But the disorganized way in which they are scattered over the surface is at odds with the prevailing ethos for order – and even with the precision of the stitching in the rest of this quilt. Was this some desperate attempt to break away from conformity, perhaps an undercover bid for self-expression in conventional quiltmaking?

The strips, running horizontally in this quilt, are decorated with the local patterns: all the white strips bear the Plait, while the red strips alternate between the Worm and the Weardale Chain. The patterns can also be seen on the other side of the quilt, opposite.

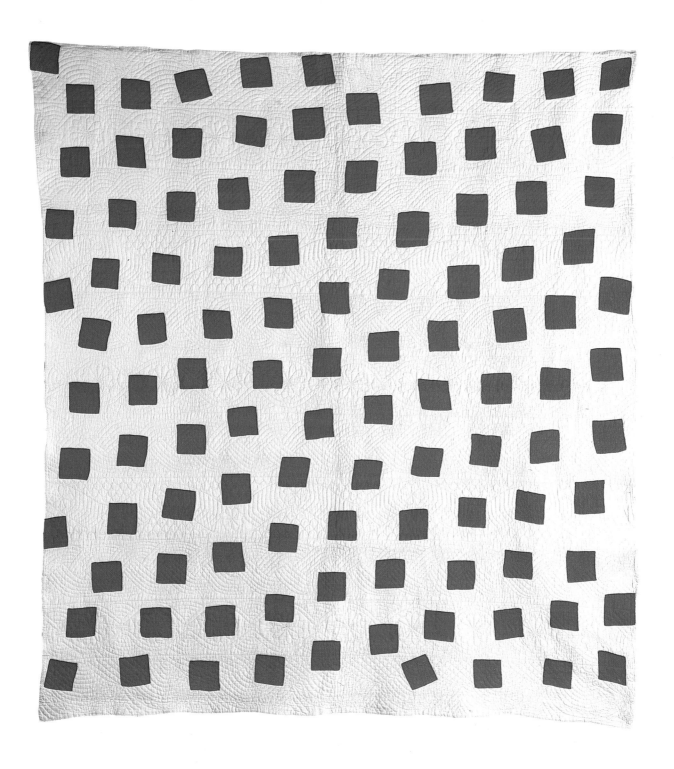

Hand sewn cotton, filled with cotton wadding and hand quilted.
English. Early 20th century. 234 × 218cm (92 × 86in).

◆ Colourwash Studies ◆

Deirdre Amsden's idyllic colourwash series epitomizes the English quiltmaking tradition in an entirely original way. Reversing the convention of using shape to build pattern, she dissolves the patch shapes in the overall image. She uses square patches only, and a spectrum of colourful cotton lawn prints, but neither of these elements is obvious in the 'painting' that results when they are pieced together. Each fabric has a distinct identity, but Deirdre Amsden deploys it only as an abstraction of colour and light. The patches are graded tonally in a series of exercises. Each scatters the image in the print and creates a colour composition; sharp contrasts of light and dark lend formal strength to the quilts but, elsewhere, dissolve into soft pointillist patterns.

If her work seems simply pretty, look again. Each piece is painstakingly planned and prepared. In order to see how the patches relate, Deirdre Amsden will use a reducing glass to concentrate her pattern and make any imbalance more glaringly evident. She works in minute detail, creating small, exquisite wallhangings. Their design is further textured with quilting patterns carved into the coloured surface.

The quilts

Top Left A disciplined design, with hard-edged contrasts of light and dark patterns at opposite corners establishing a frame, but also suggesting different light sources and creating an interplay of surfaces. The central area has curvilinear quilting, but the border is quilted with simple diagonals.

Top Right Gradation of colour and tone from light to dark is demonstrated in seven rich and subtly different ways. The dark and light ends of the strips alternate across the quilt in a series of contrasts. The tones break down and merge at the centre, softening the rigidity of the strips and the darker areas seem to come forward off the surface of the quilt.

Bottom Left In the least static of the designs, swirling lines of quilting spread outwards like ripples on a lake. They are most densely concentrated on the paler areas of the pattern, making it recede. This band of lighter, more fragmented colour drifts across the quilt diagonally, while darker colours and heavier patterns, ridged with rays of wider quilting, gravitate towards opposite corners.

Bottom Right A framed design echoes the first quilt, with strong light-dark contrasts lying horizontally.

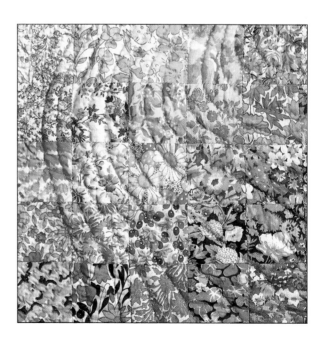

Detail of the third quilt, bottom left, opposite, showing the swirling lines of the quilting stitches that literally add another dimension to all of these quilts. Deirdre Amsden sees the quilting pattern as at least as much of a challenge as the patchwork itself, and is always interested in exploring the quilting potential of whole-cloth quilts (see her designs on pp120–1).

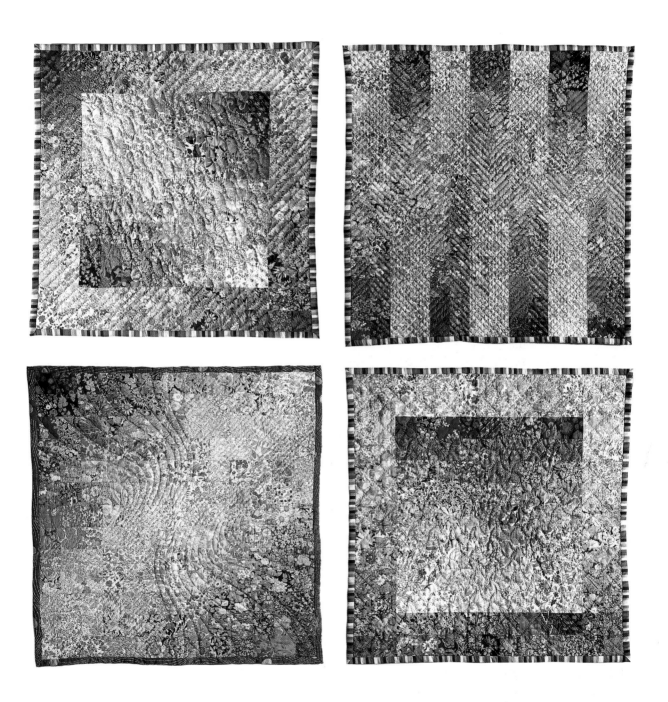

Machine stitched cotton lawn patches, filled with polyester wadding and hand quilted with silk thread.
English. 1981–85. Each quilt 53 × 53cm (21 × 21in). Deirdre Amsden.

◆ Military Quilt ◆

Men in the armed services have always been adept at needlework: mending uniforms, knitting, and making small objects to while away the time when there was nothing much to do and they were far from home. In Britain, men have traditionally taken part in the family quiltmaking effort, often designing the whole quilt as well as cutting the templates and the fabric patches, and even helping to sew them together. So there is nothing surprising about the existence of military quilts.

Quilts of this type were popular in the 1850s and 1860s, though this particular example may date from around the time of the Boer War (1899–1902). Some were made by professional tailors, using pieces left over from uniforms and mess jacket facings, but they were often made by wounded men during convalescence. The practice continued up to World War II, when patchwork pieces were included in the parcels of various handicrafts sent to prisoners of war.

Organization with panache

Uniform fabrics are stiff, thick and heavy to work, and the quilts made by the wounded were generally much simpler in design. This brilliantly conceived and executed piece was more probably the work of several men under the organizing genius of someone whose military precision was coupled with considerable artistic flair.

Strictly speaking, it is a coverlet, rather than a quilt, since no stitching holds the top and backing together. At first glance it may seem simple, but this is no product of a military plodder: only five colours are used, but the proportions are well balanced, and the result is colourful and vibrant. There is a fine sense of scale, with smaller patches making a true mosaic in the centre squares and more substantial patches in the bold, clear border. Combined with the diagonal set of the patches, these proportions bring movement and liveliness into a highly disciplined geometric design.

Detail of the quilt centre (top) where the star motif is a focal point. The tiny patches, only 2cm (¾in) square, have rounded edges where the fabric refuses to lie flat. The incongruous backing (left) seems to belong more to the world of the colonel's lady.

Hand stitched woollen uniform fabrics.
English. c 1900. 221 × 221cm (87 × 87in).

REPEATED BLOCK DESIGNS

The making of a patchwork top using a series of repeated blocks was a style unique to America, although the technique was introduced there by the early European settlers. It was an economical and effective way of using scraps of fabric. In the case of block patterns, a number of patches were sewn together into a square or, more rarely, a rectangle, and when enough blocks had been made they could be joined together to make a complete top.

The method was relatively quick and it was also space saving. Each block could be worked individually and a large area was involved only at the end, when the blocks were joined together and quilted. As the name of the best known block pattern, Log Cabin, suggests, the best quilts often originated in the most modest and cramped surroundings.

The blocks can either be separated from each other with lattice strips or be joined together to make an overall design in which the individuality of each block is lost. Within each block, the arrangement can be symmetrical, producing the same pattern no matter how the block is placed, or asymmetrical, offering greater design potential. Most block patterns were based on a simple division of a square: the templates were made by folding squares of paper and cutting the shapes from card. Patterns were exchanged through communal gatherings such as agricultural fairs and, of course, at quilting bees – social events, usually held in the spring, at which the patchworks made during the long winter months were quilted.

Although such quilts were not intended to be hung, the makers intuitively planned them to be seen as a whole. The block technique revolutionized quilt design and quiltmaking and, as can be seen here, continues to inspire innovative designs.

♦ Four Winds & Delectable Mountains ♦

Here are two quilts made towards the end of the last century. Very different in feeling, each expresses the success of the functional approach to design that Americans perfected in their utility quilts. They also share the strong personality that red contributes to a design, whether it is against a dark or a light background. But most importantly, they demonstrate very strikingly how the character of a repeating block may vary. In one quilt the block emerges strongly owing to its relative isolation. In the second, the true potential of a block is realized, as the individual block is submerged into a much stronger overall design.

Four Winds

Also known as Star of the West, the plain wools, black ground and stark simplicity of design confirm this to be a Canadian Mennonite quilt of the 1880s.

The woollen fabrics absorb the light: the black, in particular, has taken on a mysterious depth. It exaggerates the glowing, advancing qualities of the 'demonic' red shapes. The bold motif stands out aggressively against the bottomless black ground.

Each block is pieced, using straight and curved seams. Contour quilting outlines the shapes and a separate quilting pattern of concentric rings links the blocks together.

Delectable Mountains

Even in its name, this variation on a traditional quilt design presents a contrast with the energy of the Mennonite quilt. The delectable mountains were symbols of peace and plenty in Bunyan's *Pilgrim's Progress*; the early settlers gave many patterns names of religious significance.

The rich effect of this work is achieved by a multiplication of relatively small, five-patch blocks, each divided diagonally into a light half – a plain white triangle – and a darker half – a slightly smaller triangle with rows of smaller triangles forming a sawtooth edge along the two shorter sides.

The planning, cutting and stitching for such a quilt is immensely complicated, and the maker must have been experienced. The four central blocks were probably put together first so that the red halves met, then the composite square grew progressively bigger with added rows of blocks. At the outside edge, half-blocks were added as fillers. Two separate strip borders complete the design.

Unlike the deep black of Four Winds, the pale ground of this quilt has the effect of diluting the red, making it less assertive.

Delectable Mountains. Hand stitched and quilted cotton fabrics and filling. American. Late 19th century. 205 × 185cm (82 × 73in).

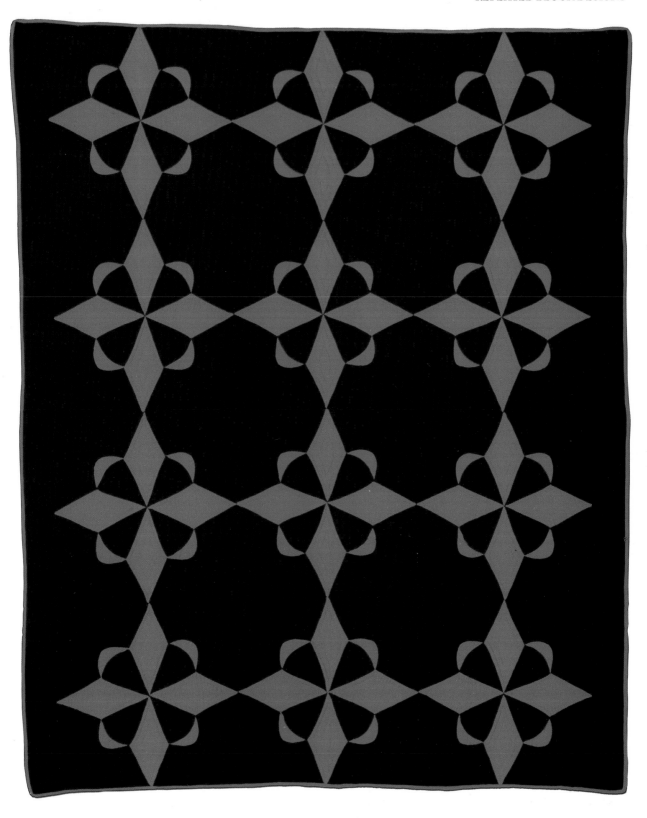

Four Winds. Hand stitched and quilted wool.
Canadian Mennonite. 1880. 194 × 162cm (76 × 64in).

◆ Silk Chequerboard ◆

The Log Cabin pattern is a classic, and deservedly popular among quiltmakers because of its versatility. Its straight-sided strips are satisfactorily quick to piece together and can be cut either from tiny scraps or from fabrics specially bought for the purpose. The strips are sewn in a clockwise direction round a centre square, black in this example but commonly red, to signify the hearth fire in the cabin (see pp 68–9). The square blocks are divided diagonally into a triangle of light-toned strips and a triangle of dark-toned ones, affording a very wide range of patterns, only limited once the blocks are set together.

Luxury fabrics

Although early examples of Log Cabin have been found in Europe, the pattern is most closely associated with the early settlers of America, for whom it provided an economical use of scrap fabrics combined with great creative potential. This quilt, however, dates from the latter part of the Victorian era, when the pattern had become gentrified and was used, like crazy quilts, as a vehicle for the display of silks and satins. It might have been intended to lie artistically on top of a bed, but was more probably made as a drape for a drawing room.

Some of the strips appear to have been made from ribbon fabric and have stood the test of time quite well; other strips are now beginning to rot, possibly owing to the chemical finish used to give body to delicate dress silks.

Colour and texture

This whole piece speaks of leisure, luxury and conspicuous consumption, but it is not just a display of wealth: the maker used her fabrics for an exercise in texture and colour. She contrasted the luminosity of the rich silks with the matt black velvet of the centre squares, and used an astonishing range of sparkling colours from dragonfly blue to spanking white and imperial purple.

The sumptuous red velvet border shares the light and dark tones of the silk interior, according to the fall of the light, while its glowing ruby colour draws out the reds in the body of the design but still frames and unites the whole multicoloured area.

The Chequerboard arrangement of the blocks is a common Log Cabin variant; in this quilt, though, the dark tones of the centre squares represents a departure from the traditional red or yellow. It still provides a focal point but the block no longer needs the homely fireside image, and the piece as a whole has something of the translucent quality of stained glass.

This detail shows how the three-dimensional quality of Log Cabins is exaggerated by the use of tonal gradations and the graded lengths of the strips, making the centres seem deeply inset.

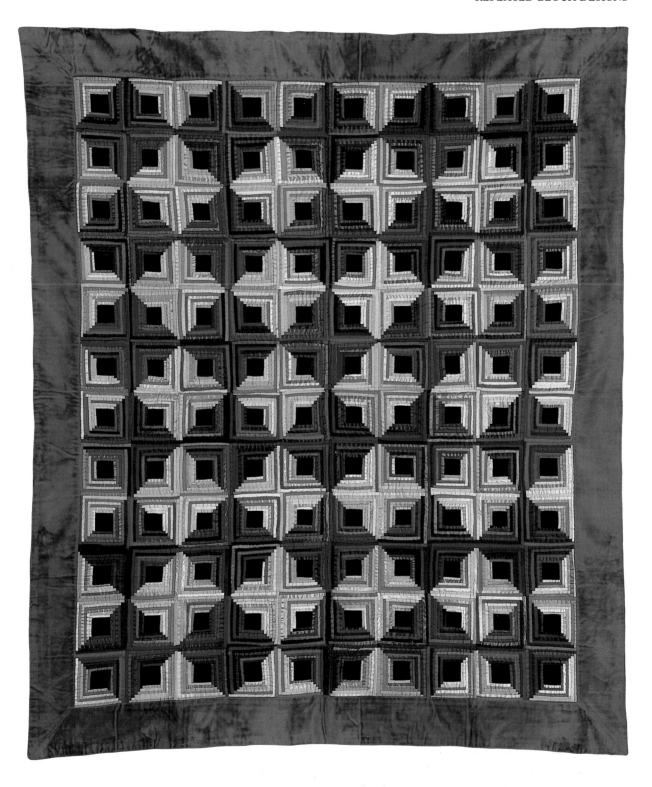

Hand stitched silks and velvets. Coverlet.
English. 1880. 179 × 155cm (70½ × 61in).

◆ Dancing Tulips ◆

This quilt was made for decoration rather than just warmth. The maker has endowed her appliqué tulips with a character of their own: they appear to sway in the breeze, a feeling reinforced by the way the design has been reversed from row to row.

Pennsylvanian quilts

The tulip motif was brought to America, along with other simple, colourful images,

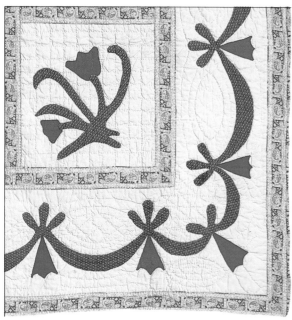

by the large numbers of German settlers who fled religious persecution and political upheaval, arriving in the New World, especially in Pennsylvania, between 1683 and 1775.

Many of them were superb needlewomen and because they tended to live in self-contained religious communities they maintained a clearly recognizable visual tradition, using bright colours – reds, greens, oranges and pinks – and pictorial motifs such as tulips. Swag borders were also a popular feature of their quilts.

Confident choice of fabrics

The fabrics of this quilt have been pleasantly and sensitively arranged by someone who had obviously already made a number of quilts and was confident in her choice of suitable fabrics. She has picked a very small geometric floral print for the greenery and a plain red for the flowers.

Each tulip block is contained within lattice strips cut from a paisley printed fabric that echoes the curved shapes of the tulips and the swag border. Paisley patterned fabrics were popular quite early in the 19th century, though this quilt was probably made around 1850. This is very much a 'best' quilt and the fabric was almost certainly specially bought.

When looked at closely, each tulip stem and its accompanying leaves appear to have been cut in one piece. The effect is not very graceful, but this slight clumsiness is submerged when the quilt is viewed from a distance and the motifs seen in repeat.

The flower baskets have probably been included in the swag border to add interest to the side view of the quilt when in use. Although different in feeling to the tulips, they are characteristic of Pennsylvanian designs.

The swag border, reflecting the tulip theme, has been beautifully stitched and the corner turn is handled skilfully so that the design is uninterrupted.

Hand stitched and quilted cotton fabric.
American. c 1850. 225 × 225cm (89 × 89in).

◆ Friendship Medley ◆

Album or autograph quilts, which were popular during the second half of the last century, were lovingly stitched as a token of affection, often as a leaving present for someone departing from a community. The general rule was that each block should be made by the person who signed it, from her own material. Album quilts could be pieced or appliquéd; some have Bible texts or sentimental verses included. When the individual blocks had all been pieced, a party would be held to stitch them together.

This particular quilt, in a design usually known as Friendship Medley, is something of a mystery. The blocks are all hand stitched and signed and dated over a period from 1882 to 1900. All are patchwork, a few are repeated and most have 'Wakefield New Hampshire' embroidered on them.

The makers appear to have been unusually elderly, several being 96 and 98 years old, which may explain the uncharacteristically imperfect workmanship. Many album quilts are exquisite in both design and stitching, the makers vying with each other to produce their best. Here, however, not only is the stitching uneven but there are a good many somewhat unruly squares – maybe the result of failing eyesight. Possibly this is a Grandmother's Quilt.

Ohio Star (top) and Star. Two of the 63 blocks that make up this album quilt. Ohio Star is one of several which suggest family connections: it is embroidered 'Great Grand Ma Frances Smith 1882'. However, most of the blocks are formally signed 'Mrs' or a Christian name, suggesting that neighbours and friends also helped.

Blocks, row by row
1 Ohio Star, Hour Glass, Crazy, Variable Star, 9-Patch, Album, Birds in Flight; 2 Pinwheel, Crazy, Squares, Bear's Paw, Tumbler, 9-Patch with Crazy centre, Log Cabin;
3 9-Patch, Turkey Tracks, 8-Pointed Star, Broken Dishes, Log Cabin, Chimney Sweep, Birds in Flight; 4 Ohio Star, Diamond in Square, Pineapple Log Cabin, Album, Oklahoma Sunburst (Sunflower), Ohio Star, Iowa Star;
5 Pinwheel, Lattice, Odd Fellows, Ohio Star, Odd Fellows, Hexagons, 9-Patch; 6 Album, Indian Star, 6-Pointed Star, Star, Rising Star, Crazy, Log Cabin; 7 Crazy, Log Cabin, Evening Star, Hexagon Star, Churn Dash, Churn Dash (Monkey Wrench or Hole in the Barn Door), Crazy;
8 Album, Hexagon, Chimney Sweep (Christian Cross), Crazy, Broken Dishes, Goose Tracks variation, 9-Patch;
9 Log Cabin, Letter 'S', Squares, Crown and Thorns, Chimney Sweep, Odd Fellows, Chimney Sweep

Hand stitched cotton blocks joined together by machine.
American. c 1900. 244 × 194cm (96 × 76in).

◆ Railroad Crossing & Irish Chain ◆

These two quilts both use a basic chain type pattern, alternating a nine-patch block with a plain square set diagonally and, in the case of Railroad Crossing, an additional block. With the controlled use of colour and a highly disciplined lattice grid pattern, the quilts cannot be described as pretty, but each is visually pleasing and shows a simple, unfussy approach to design.

Railroad Crossing

This is a most unusual design. It uses a pattern composed of a nine-patch block, a plain white square and a second pieced block called Garden of Eden. The most interesting feature of this design is the way the large white squares 'eat' into the corners of the larger pieced blocks which at first glance appear to be appliquéd. The grid of indigo blue and grey squares is subtly relieved by the occasional placing of pink patches and more noticeable yellow ones around the edges. Perhaps the maker did not have

enough fabric and hoped that these patches would not show over the edge of the bed?

The quilting in the white squares follows the cross shape of the Garden of Eden block. Elsewhere it follows the shapes of the individual square patches.

The pattern would have been put together in diagonal strips or rows, the rows of Garden of Eden and the nine-patch block alternating with rows of plain white squares and the nine-patch. A simple blue-patterned binding finishes the edge.

Irish Chain

This is a single version of the ever-popular Irish Chain pattern, which can also be used in a double or treble version. The basic nine-patch block, using indigo and white printed fabric, is set on its point with alternating plain white squares. The pattern is framed with a sawtooth border (in which the maker has obviously had some difficulty turning the corners, having to squeeze the patches in as best she could) and completed with a solid frame.

This quilt is particularly satisfying to touch. The pieced top is densely quilted all over with a small square grid pattern, giving it a crisp, textured feel. Such plain, large squares must be well quilted if they are not to wrinkle and look empty.

The popularity of Irish Chain patterns probably stems from the fact that they were easy to make up, did not require too much patchwork and used squares only.

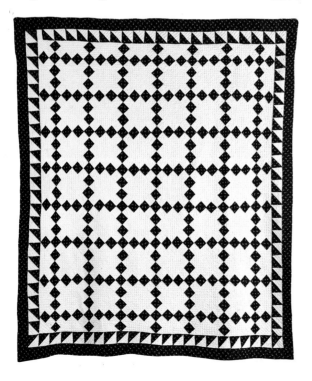

Irish Chain. Hand stitched and quilted cotton fabric. American. c 1880. 218 × 198cm (86 × 78in).

Railroad Crossing. Hand stitched and quilted cotton fabric.
American. c 1880. 203 × 178cm (80 × 70in).

◆ Colour Variations ◆

This is a set of my own designs, based on geometric shapes developed from cutting up coloured papers and rearranging them into patterns. With earlier quilts, I had always worked out my designs on graph paper, but I found this exacting and sometimes stultifying; the freedom of this method using cut paper gave some unpredictable results that were an exciting departure.

I made all but one of the designs in miniature first, using small scale templates and cutting patches from the proposed fabric. In this way, the usual jump from graph paper colours to the reality of fabric was avoided. In addition, I found that the method allowed much more flexibility.

Razzmatazz *(top left)*

I like the spontaneity of the design and the dynamic effect of the vivid colours on the dark ground of this first quilt. The colours appear luminous and magical, shining against the deep black and evoking excitement and mystery.

The positive black spaces give strength to the shafts of bright light and the strong diagonal lines suggest movement. Explosive outbursts occurring intermittently across the surface emphasize a tremendous jungle-like life force. The diagonal flow of the yellow breaks up the symmetry of the warm concentration of colours at the centre and the cooler, darker colours around them.

Birds of Paradise *(top right)*

In the next quilt I arranged the pieces with a strong warm/cold contrast in the centre and relieved the monotony of the previous black ground by using tints and shades of cool blues, purples and greens.

Banana Split *(bottom left)*

For the third quilt, I experimented with fabric placed on layers of clear acetate so that I could build up the design and change the background without disrupting the whole pattern. I used a background of graded yellows to light the piece from behind, putting the diagonal shapes in shadow.

Untitled quilt *(bottom right)*

The first and last quilts are, in a colour sense, reversed. In this one the bright, luminous colours so evident in 'Razzmatazz' are just seen as occasional glints through the undergrowth. However, I consider this to be the least successful of the series: some of the spontaneity of the original has been lost.

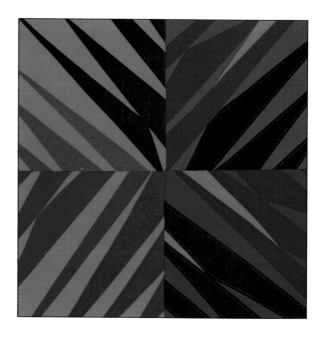

The sewing technique for all the quilts shown opposite was the same: an individual template was made for each shape; these were then pieced into large square blocks and machine quilted, following the lines of the patches, to foundation squares of cotton domett.

The detail shown above is from 'Birds of Paradise', opposite, top right.

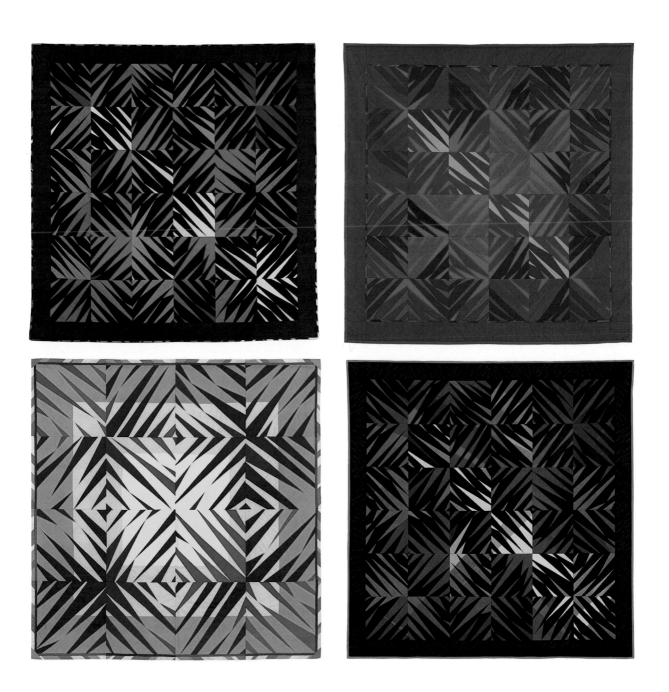

Machine stitched and quilted cotton. Layers tied in by hand. English. 1981–5.
'Banana Split' (bottom left) 110 × 110cm (43 × 43in).
All other quilts 171 × 171cm (67 × 67in).
Michele Walker

◆ Robbing Peter to Pay Paul ◆

This four-patch block design is usually made in two contrasting colours. A patch is 'robbed' from one coloured fabric and compensated with a patch from the second, and vice versa, giving a positive – negative repeat.

The biblical connotation of the name is typical of many old Quaker patterns. A similar design using the same 'robbing' principle is Melon Patch.

Rhythmic repetition

An unvarying block repeat can, according to mood, appeal for its soothing regularity or irritate by its predictability. In the same way, a combination of pink and blue may seem subtle or insipid, delicate or drab according to taste. Tonally, these two primaries are evenly balanced: the contrast lies in the warm and cold character of the colours rather than in any difference of lightness or darkness. There is a satisfactory tension between the meticulous shapes in warm reddish-pink and cool powdery blue. The red, characteristically, stands out against the blue, which fades to become a luminous background extending beyond the main design to frame the coloured area.

The odd number of pattern repeats running down the quilt gives a more satisfying symmetry than the even number running across, yet the pattern is so understated that this imbalance hardly impinges.

The same pattern repeat in a more extreme contrast of colour or of tone – or even in black and white – would be more dramatic, but the interaction between the blocks would remain limited, the overall pattern essentially static. By fragmenting the patch shapes and playing with a broader range of the two basic colours – perhaps paler tints and darker shades of the red and blue here, together with tones of intermediate violet – an exciting sense of colour movement across the quilt's surface might be created.

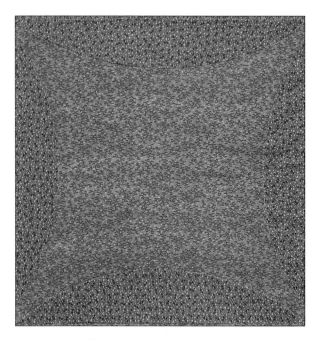

The careful quiltmaker

However, this quilt is pleasing more as a piece of good craftsmanship than for its striking design qualities. It is relatively lightweight, being made from cotton dress fabrics, their plainness relieved by the slight texturing of a minute figured pattern.

The understated effect of these two fabrics is typical of the accomplished but cautious quiltmaker whose confidence lies in her sewing rather than her creative skills. She must have been a practised needlewoman, able to machine stitch the exacting pattern of curved seams with great expertise. The fine cottons keep the curves well defined and neat, making the result look deceptively simple. As you would expect, the feather quilting around the edges and the flower motifs in the squares are intricate and neat.

When looking at this detail, remember that each shape had to be cut from a template including the seam allowance and very precisely worked in order to lie flat. The method of working is to join all the pieces first in blocks and then in rows.

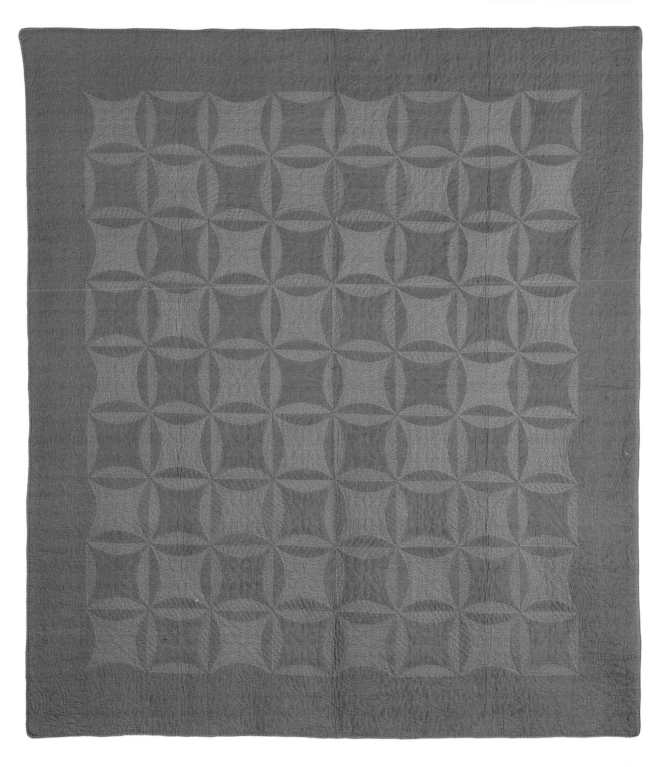

Machine stitched and hand quilted cotton fabrics.
Early 20th century. 227 × 203cm (89 × 80in).

◆ Turkey Tracks ◆

Appliqué quilts became widely popular in the middle of the last century when fabrics became more readily available, although they were usually kept for best. This particular appliqué block was originally called Wandering Foot and carried a superstition that any child, especially a boy, who slept under a quilt of this type would grow up discontented and become a wanderer. Not surprisingly, the name was later changed to Turkey Tracks.

English Turkey Tracks

This highly idiosyncratic version of the Turkey Tracks block, combined with lattice strips and a vigorous zigzag border, looks like the work of someone who had seen the American pattern and was trying to reconstruct it from memory.

The eau de nil green, red and white makes a traditional colour combination, and the border is typical of Pennsylvania, but if you look closely you can see a rose quilted among the curves, a variation of a typical North of England quilting pattern called Weardale Chain. This, together with the close, crisp nature of the quilting, indicates the English origin of the quilt. In an American quilt, there would almost certainly have been a 16-block repeat instead of the nine outsize blocks used in this quilt.

Each block consists of red turkey legs with claw feet; they have been worked by an enthusiast with scant regard for accuracy of pattern or patch. The feet vary a good deal and look like naïve drawings of palm trees or hands, and are not always positioned very carefully in the squares. The lattice strips with their plain square intersections, however, provide a certain degree of uniformity and order.

The very fine North Country quilting runs right across the main appliqué pattern, disregarding its contours. There is an interesting contrast between the cheerful but slapdash appliqué work and the meticulous and skilful quilting.

This quilt, in spite of its faults or perhaps even because of them, has enormous character and vigour, an endearing simplicity and a sense of humour.

American Turkey Tracks

This delicate and finely worked, though rather worn, quilt with its attractive swag border shows what the Turkey Track pattern conventionally looks like. It is far removed from the naïve, childlike simplicity of the other piece, but although it is neater and more accurate and has a pretty, feminine air about it, it lacks the exuberant charm of the other quilt.

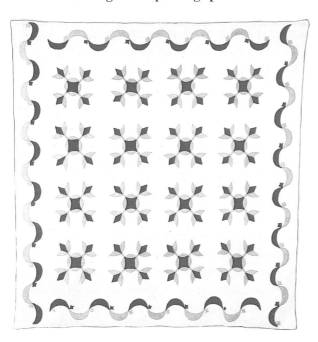

American Turkey Tracks. Hand stitched and quilted cotton fabrics. Late 19th century. 190 × 190cm (76 × 76in).

English Turkey Tracks. Hand stitched and quilted cotton fabrics.
Early 20th century. 224 × 214cm (88 × 84in).

◆ Contained Crazy ◆

Contemporary quiltmakers have recently turned back to the crazy quilt, exploring its potential as a springboard for ideas. This sophisticated and highly urbane design is by Jan Myers, a professional quiltmaker from Minneapolis, USA. Although a self-taught quiltmaker, she has a background of drawing and painting. All her work is pieced and quilted by machine, but she contrives to use her fabric colours as freely as though she were choosing from a wide-ranging palette of paints.

The underlying theme of all her work is that of colour and light and she hand-dyes all her fabrics (with procion dyes), using no printed patterns at all. The dyeing process allows her to achieve as great a subtlety and gradation of colour as if she were actually mixing paints.

In other quilts, her colours have been so delicately modulated across the quilt's surface, using single-shape patches, that they create the illusion of shadows moving across a landscape. In this quilt, however, she has departed from her usual practice of integrating colour and light on a single plane and, instead, has picked upon different patchwork devices to deal with light in a much more fragmented way, and she has used a narrower range of colours than usual.

New light on tradition

Following her inclination to respect patchwork tradition, Jan Myers has formed her crazy blocks from intricate pieces, apparently random in shape and size. Their colour, however, is deliberately controlled and although the lattice strips are uniform in size and colour, the squares that mark their intersections vary subtly in tone from palest mauve to dark maroon.

This superimposition of a grid over the lower plane of crazy blocks gives the illusion of a third dimension. Within this frame-

work, Jan Myers explores the relationship between colour and light on two separate but related visual planes. Towards the centre, where the crazy patches darken, rather like the eye of the storm, the grid seems to be raised off the surface. Gradually, the crazy patches lighten in tone and the grid becomes submerged around the edges, as the colour contrasts balance themselves out.

The crazy blocks encompass a wide range of tonal gradations, including pinks, browns, blues and purples, yet all are based on related but muted tones of a very limited red-blue axis. The relatively small scale of the piece gives the design a concentrated and visually intense quality, exploiting colour harmonies and the angularity of the patches.

The border gathers all the elements of the quilt into a sort of order, echoing the crazy blocks in a pleasingly deliberate way.

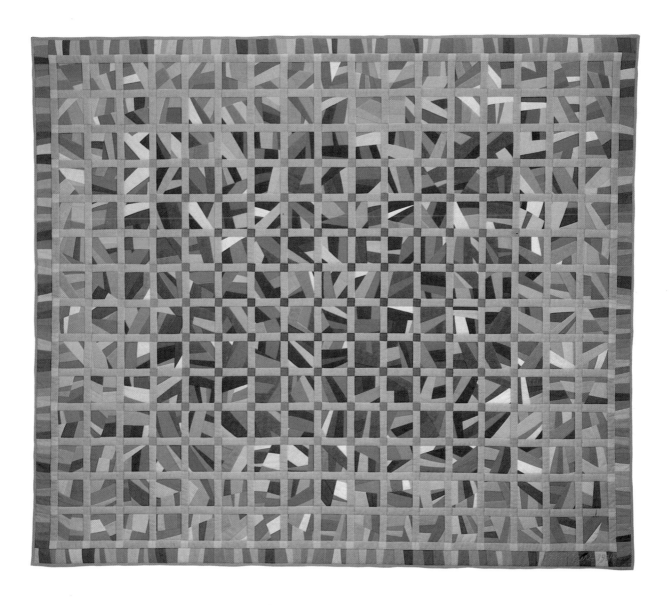

Machine pieced and quilted, hand-dyed cotton muslin.
American. 1984. 145 × 124cm (57 × 49in). Jan Myers.

◆ Straight Furrow & Barn Raising ◆

One of the attractions of the Log Cabin technique is the wide range of patterns that are created when blocks are set together. The names given to these patterns were taken from the everyday experiences of the American settlers: Barn Raising, for example, resembled the laid out sections of a barn before it was built while Straight Furrow echoed the lines of a ploughed field.

Straight Furrow

In this sophisticated quilt, the black diagonals appear to be raised up from the surface to form railings behind which lies a random design of soft colours. It is this unexpected and seemingly illogical placement of cool greys with bursts of warm yellow and pinkish beige, similar to natural outcroppings of rock, that holds the eye and invites serious attention.

The strips are narrow, giving a smoother diagonal flow than usual, and the blue centre squares have faded so that they blend in with the design instead of providing highlights, as the maker originally intended.

Many traditional quilts show a mistake, deliberately created to avoid competing with God's perfection. In this case, two pink strips and a light grey one lie in a dark grey area in the seventh block from the top on the right side.

Barn Raising

This pattern is very different in feeling and design from the plain, muted, light hues and strong, albeit faded, dark tones of Straight Furrow. Here, the feminine, patterned fabrics often break up the continuity, especially in the dark areas, and the red centre squares are too small and remain almost unnoticed in the medley of printed fabrics. The yellowness of the lighter fabrics illuminates the design and contrasts well with the blues.

ABOVE *This detail of the floral, decorative backing shows how different in feeling it is from the front of the quilt, although it has been brought round to make a self-bound edge.*

LEFT *Barn Raising. Hand stitched cotton fabrics. English. c 1875. 235 × 229cm (92½ × 90in).*

Straight Furrow. Hand stitched woollen and suiting fabrics. Layers tied together.
American. c 1880. 197 × 177cm (77½ × 69½in).

◆ Stripy Step & Pyramid in Disguise ◆

Her distinctive style and painstaking crafts-manship have made Pauline Burbidge one of Britain's most notable quiltmakers. Her quilts are made for beds or walls, but need to be seen from a distance to reveal their full complexity. Although her design ideas are continually changing, her technique has re-mained constant since she started quilting. Each design is worked out beforehand with the utmost precision and the quilts are machine pieced and quilted (see also pp118–19). She works with fabrics in solid colours, now predominantly using commer-cially dyed Hunan silk. Her quilts are filled with a dense cotton wadding that gives weight but little bulk to the surface.

Stripy Step

The design of this quilt is concerned with the metamorphosis of three-dimensional images into stripes and flat patterns. The eye is first drawn diagonally across the design, only to be interrupted and drawn back by the lines of stripes and the quilting pattern, which travel in opposite directions.

The solid architectural quality suggested by the overall design exists in a space of constantly changing levels. The border is integrated into the design, extending it out-wards rather than acting as a frame. Similar-ly, the quilting pattern is fully integrated with the patchwork, emphasizing the diagonal flow and texturing the plain surface of the quilt.

Pyramid in Disguise

Again, Pauline Burbidge has made use of tone to emphasize the three-dimensional aspect of her design. For the first time she has considered the reverse of the quilt in the over-all design, with the crazy pattern of the front repeated on a larger scale and in the opposite corner of the reverse, with the three large shapes echoing the repeat block pattern.

TOP 'Pyramid in Disguise'. 1985. 183 × 168cm (72 × 66in). All other details as in 'Stripy Step'.
ABOVE The reverse of the quilt shows how it has been made in two halves, with a diagonal seam.

'Stripy Step'. Machine stitched and quilted Hunan silk and cotton wadding.
English. 1984. 180 × 168cm (71 × 66in). Pauline Burbidge

◆ Ontario & Mennonite Crazy Quilts ◆

Crazy quilts originally evolved as a way of making the best possible use of every scrap left over from clothes making. The random shapes were overlapped and stitched onto a foundation material and the raw edges were then covered with feather stitching.

Between 1875 and 1900, the Victorians embraced the technique and produced work so embroidered, embellished and decorated, and so encrusted with various silks, velvets, brocades, beads, ribbons, sequins, bow ties and even hat bands as to be grotesque rather than crazy.

Ontario Crazy

Like the other crazy quilt shown here, this piece has a certain discipline, showing what some might term the acceptable face of 'craziness'. The framework, consisting of square blocks, imparts a welcome sense of order to the design.

This piece is unusual in that it is quilted.

Usually the elaborately worked top (which often included heavy woollens and suiting fabrics) and the lining were sufficiently warm without an interlining. The contrast stitching around the patches gives coherence to the shapes in this pleasing quilt, which was probably intended as a functional bedcover rather than a decorative sofa throw.

Mennonite Crazy

This quilt was also made as a working bedcover and its dark grid of banding gives it the discipline that a crazy quilt needs if it is to avoid total anarchy. The black polished cotton banding and quilting pattern, known as 'eggs', is common in the American Mid-West, though the use of fine wools, darker colours and frames around squares of odd-shaped pieces is typical of Mennonite quilts from Illinois. The rich deep red border and embroidered embellishments are an echo of the high Victorian tradition.

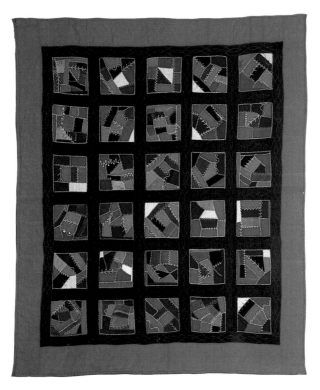

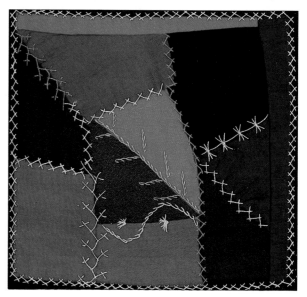

Mennonite Crazy. Hand stitched polished cotton, fine woollens and suitings. Embroidered and quilted. American. c 1910. 206 × 180cm (81 × 71in). The detail shows the embroidery that conceals seams and decorates some patches.

Ontario Crazy. Hand stitched and quilted wool, velvet, suiting and tweed.
Canadian. c 1900. 200 × 168cm (78 × 66in).

◆ Blue Undercurrents & La Tempête ◆

Michael James trained as a painter but developed this particular style of patchwork between 1973 and 1980. The method itself is relatively simple. Long strips of fabric of varying widths and carefully balanced tones and colours are machine stitched together to create a new fabric. Shapes are then cut from this and pieced together in the usual way. The templates are simple shapes based on a square, with curves introduced to give a fluidity and rhythm that is not possible with straight seams.

The strip-pieced fabrics are made on the basis of selections from what amounts to a filing system of colour graded cottons, and although you may occasionally notice a small anonymous spotted or striped print that has been used to add visual texture, most of the fabrics used are plain colours.

The method may be simple but the designs are not: their subtle complexities and precision, the confident use of colour and the relationship between the curved and straight lines are worked out with considerable skill and the results are satisfying and painterly.

Both pieces shown here are quilted in the seams so that the stitches are hidden but the contours and colours are accentuated. These quilts could be taken for details of a grander vision, the lines reaching the edge of the work as though continuing beyond it.

Blue Undercurrents

This is one of a series of quilts that show a constant tidal movement across the surface, where the colours and design continually threaten to break their bounds, practically submerging the underlying square grid. There is a balance between the deep, dark spaces and the light, warm colours that dance backwards and forwards and work in opposite directions, like the influx and undertow of the tide on a rocky shore. In addition, the colour values are graded to enhance the feeling of space and depth.

The technique uses the square block as a repeated unit, relying on the interaction between the blocks to create the design. The result is an abstract, asymmetrical composition, the curved seams of which add sensuality, which is further enhanced by the tactile quality of the fabrics.

La Tempête

This is another variation on a sea theme but in this piece the light and dark contrast is used to create a somewhat grander image of wind and storm. The whites and pale colours flow with some purpose towards the top of the quilt, with little spurts of energy directed off to the left. The central action is curved, though the basic square blocks are more obvious nearer the edges of the quilt.

'La Tempête'. Machine pieced and quilted cotton and cotton wadding. American. 1983. 221 × 200cm (87 × 79in). Michael James.

'Blue Undercurrents'. Machine pieced and quilted cotton and cotton wadding.
American. 1983.178 × 178cm (70 × 70in). Michael James.

◆ Star Trees & Goose in Pond ◆

These two quilts are typical of those made by the settlers for everyday use. Both are hand stitched in plain cottons, making use of the ever-popular white and red. They are then filled with cotton wadding and quilted. A comparison of the two shows the striking contrast in effect between the designs of two individuals working in the same tradition and with similar materials.

Star Trees

This quiltmaker has taken a traditional pattern and turned it into her own, using an eight-pointed star as the basis and putting the tree trunk where the bottom two star points would have been.

The blocks are deliberately isolated from one another by the strong grid of red lattice strips, each with a contrasting blue square at the intersection. Yet the maker's military precision seems to have let her down somewhat, where the bottom lattice strips fail to line up.

The quilting is straightforward and functional, made up of just enough diagonal lines to keep the wadding in place during washing. These are more closely placed on the white areas, but the maker has put most of her creative energies into working the blocks themselves. The result is a vigorous all-over design whose bold shapes and intensity of colour stop just short of crudeness.

Goose in Pond

Whereas the Star Trees are a direct, though simple, representation of a natural image, Goose in Pond is more abstract. Triangles were often used to represent goose or turkey tracks, or birds in flight.

This quilt is another example of the way a quiltmaker would put a personal interpretation on a traditional block. Generally this is a five-patch pattern, but here the centre units are longer than usual. The maker certainly

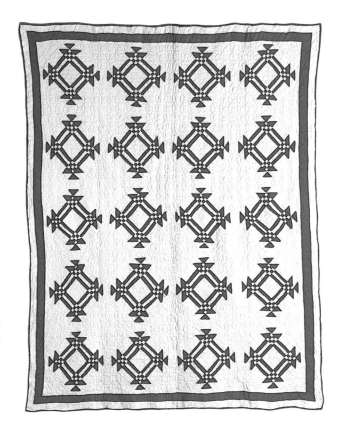

had difficulty with the points of the triangles, and the blocks would probably have been more successful if they had been set more closely together.

The isolated setting of the blocks diffuses the overall impact, and only the vigorous colour quality of the red fabric and the dense texturing of the quilting on the white ground saves the pattern from being rather bland. A firm red border holds the floating red motif in place. In contrast with Star Trees the effect of the quilt is light and almost delicate.

The plain white squares are quilted with overlapping circles, sometimes known as Wine Glass pattern.

Goose in Pond. Hand pieced and quilted cotton fabric. American. Late 19th century. 229 × 178cm (90 × 70in).

Star Trees. Hand pieced and quilted cotton.
American. Late 19th century. 179 × 169cm (70 × 66in).

◆ Diamonds and Squares ◆

In this well-known arrangement of strips in a single Log Cabin block, the different colours give an impression of two contrasting triangles. Convention has it that one corner of the cabin 'room' is illuminated by the glow from a central 'fire', represented in this quilt by Turkey-red squares, while the opposite one lies in shadow.

Overall the distribution of the triangles makes patterns of diamonds, diagonals and zigzags. When tonal contrast is extreme, the alternating light and dark shapes have an almost positive-negative impact.

Reading the patches for history

A closer look at this quilt modifies the first impression of hard-edged geometry. Even given the guidelines in the striped fabrics, the quiltmaker manifested a casual disregard for straight lines. The strips vary in width and the stripes are askew, with the charming irregularity of uneven cottage walls. This suggests the speed and artlessness with which the quilt was put together from old workshirts, flannelette and dress fabrics. Closer examination also shows variation in what seems at first a stark light-dark contrast. The predominant sugary pink varies in strength and blends with the striped shirtings.

Given this preference for plainness, the bright backing fabric is startling. Backings for utility quilts were often whatever came to hand: here, a length of cheap cotton print.

A rare survival

One of the puzzles about this quilt is that it has even survived, and is in good condition. Many of its characteristics point to a utility quilt, made quickly in a poor working household from scrap-bag fabrics. Yet for some reason it must have been stored away: there is far less disparity among the blacks than if such unstable dyes had been exposed to daylight for even a few years.

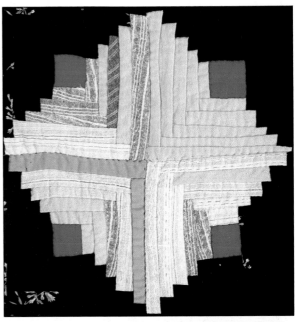

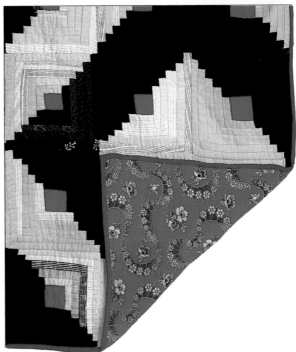

The layers of Log Cabin quilts are usually tied together but here the maker has quilted around each centre red square. It is always interesting to see the backing fabric. It is not always in keeping with the design on the front and probably not intended to be seen.

Hand stitched cotton Log Cabin blocks.
American. 1870. 205 × 170cm (81 × 67in)

SINGLE IMAGE DESIGNS

Single image quilts are those in which the design is either based on a strong central image or consists of an all-over picture, whether naturalistic or abstract, as opposed to those designs which are built up with a repeated shape or block. This wide ranging category includes whole cloth quilts which rely on the stitching to make the pattern, medallion quilts and the complex designs produced by layered appliqué. Some are intended to be viewed from a particular angle and have a very definite top and bottom to the design while others are symmetrically organized.

Medallion patterns were an early development in quiltmaking in which the design was constructed from the centre outwards. Early quilts of this nature often had an appliquéd panel at the centre surrounded by several frames. In complete contrast, the Amish quiltmakers of Pennsylvania used the bare minimum of shapes for their bold yet infinitely simple and elegant designs.

Centred images are also associated with traditional appliqué, such as the perennially popular Tree of Life design, with its strong upward flow, and with whole cloth quilts. In the latter, a dominant central design is generally surrounded by smaller motifs linked by filler patterns.

A single image quilt, however, need not rely on a centred image enclosed within a border, and some of the most exciting designs are those which ignore this rule. Dinah Prentice deliberately designs her abstract quilt pictures so that the imagination extends them beyond the edges, while Linda MacDonald's quilt refuses to conform to a centralized formula and takes the viewer instead on an exciting journey through many different levels and dimensions.

◆ Paisley Pinwheel ◆

The practice when quilting of completely ignoring the patterned and pieced design was much more common in Wales than in the North Country. In many cases, the right side of a Welsh quilt was the unpatterned cloth side on which the quilting could be plainly seen, and the patchwork, carrying with it the stigma of poverty, was used for the back, just as it was in many areas of the North of England.

Traditional Welsh patterns

The Welsh loved swirls, whorls and leaf shapes, and used the paisley shape in a quilting pattern known as the Welsh Pear. Travelling quilters had a repertoire of their own patterns and were largely responsible for the continuity of Welsh traditional patterns during the last century. The Welsh tended to quilt onto heavier fabrics, so that the pattern was deeply carved into the surface (this can be clearly seen on the quilt on page 82), and complicated designs would have been wasted.

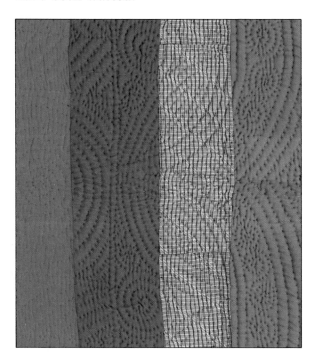

This quilt was obviously intended as a rather special, if not exactly best, bedcover; both the patchwork and the quilting have been carefully planned. The pale fawn striped fabric may have come from a waistcoat, and the paisley patterned cotton or cloth has been cut from a shawl.

Probably made around 1880, the work is an excellent example of the rather simplistic and 'sensible' attitude that the Welsh had towards quilt design.

Straightforward patchwork

To make the construction fast and easy, the patchwork is treated in the most straightforward way possible. The technique of using a large image at the centre, surrounded by a series of borders, is more often found in late 17th- and early 18th-century work, and bears a similarity to the Amish designs that came later. In American quilts, the Pinwheel is usually used as a small repeated block across the surface, not as a single image.

The textured fabrics have been quite carefully placed and the paisley and striped materials evenly distributed throughout; the whirling of the blades is accentuated by the swirling paisley design and the circular quilting pattern. The Welsh liking for strong, rich colours and bold designs is confidently handled and their traditional respect for quilting shows in the importance of the quilting pattern, which ignores the design of the pieced work.

The spiral and fan shapes of the quilting shown in this detail are typically Welsh. Spiral patterns have a close association with Celtic art and many of the quilting patterns are similar to the carved patterns that are found on Welsh love spoons.

Hand pieced and quilted paisley shawl and light woollen fabrics.
Welsh. c 1880. 200 × 181cm (79 × 71 in).

◆ Poppyfield ◆

Throughout history quilts have reflected the feelings and interests of the times in which they were made. There was a sharp decline in the craft at the turn of the century, when bedding became cheaper to buy. For a time, seduced by machine-made objects, people lost their enthusiasm and pride in those made by hand. Growing numbers of women were freed from a previously endless round of household chores and were taking jobs outside the home.

The social changes wrought by the aftermath of the First World War had a parallel effect on the art of quiltmaking. Gradually new themes and images were brought into patchwork, echoing the new technologies and changing lifestyles. In some areas, both in Britain and America, there was a revival in quiltmaking in the 1920s and 1930s, partly to provide employment during the Depression. In better off homes, however, quilting was taken up as a hobby rather than a necessity, and the older designs gave way to stronger, bolder pictorial images that were less subtle both in the quality of the stitching and in the choice of colours. Many of those new designs became an established part of the quiltmaking motifs used today.

Quiltmaking was becoming a mechanized craft; you could buy ready cut paper templates for appliquéd and pieced quilts, and there were even manufactured quilts for sale.

The emergence of quilt kits

This was the time of the blossoming of mass-produced appliqué quilt blocks, with design names such as 'Sunbonnet Sue', as well as art deco type images, such as the Fan and the Dresden Plate. Instead of hoarding scraps and inventing ways to use them up artistically, women could buy fabrics for specific designs. Themes ranged from aeroplanes (reflecting the new technology) to the traditional flowers and birds. Patterns were collected from newspapers and magazines, and ready-to-sew quilts became available in kit form – all encouraging women to sew.

Free-flowing and natural style

Appliqué was much in evidence during this period and the quilt shown here is characteristic of the larger, simplified images popular in the 1920s and 1930s. This quilt could have been designed and worked by an experienced quiltmaker or bought as a kit and sewn according to instructions.

With its popular bright colours and scalloped edges, it is particularly appealing for the flowing rhythm of the wayside flowers skilfully blended together in the large rectangular image and small centre garland. The design may have been inspired by the embroidered flowers of Hungarian folk costumes. This quilt demonstrates a very different style from earlier appliqué; it is less formal, strongly coloured and unashamedly pretty.

This detail highlights the bold and jaunty depiction of poppy, cornflower and wheatsprig in the quilt opposite. It also shows the layering technique used with more complicated appliqué.

Hand stitched and appliquéd cotton.
American. 1930. 218 × 188cm (86 × 74in).

◆ Spotted Cow ◆

Judging by its well-worn appearance, this simple country quilt has been much loved and used. It may not be a design masterpiece but it is very endearing and has several unusual features.

Welsh everyday quilts

The most striking part of this quilt is, of course, the centre panel of canvaswork – very popular in Victorian times, though not as a feature of quilts. The canvaswork picture itself is naive and not particularly finely stitched; perhaps it was made by a child who then wanted it to be used for her own quilt. The comparatively small, child's-bed size of the quilt also lends some corroboration to this idea.

In other respects, this is a typical Welsh everyday quilt, probably filled with an old blanket and made with patches of woollens, flannels and tweeds. These might have been cut from old clothes, but there is quite a wide range of fabrics and no extra-worn patches, and it is more likely that the patchwork was made from bundles bought from the local woollen mill. Such bundles were often sold pre-cut into rectangular patches and they provided an economical basis for a quilt since the new fabrics could be made into a warm, long-lasting bedcover.

Centralized design

In a quilt made from mill bundles, it was normal practice to grade the rectangular patches according to size and then arrange them into a patchwork pattern using the smallest patches at the centre and the largest around the border.

In this quilt a similar attempt has been made at a centralized design, with a strong red border round the canvaswork, echoed by the red squares at each corner of the innermost patchwork border. The larger patches have been generally used for the

outer borders, but somewhere along the line the plan broke down and an increasing number of adjustments had to be made so that the end result has a lot in common with the 'crazy' patchwork that was so popular in more well-to-do households during the late Victorian period.

The resemblance to 'crazy' work is increased by the herringbone stitching that joins the patches, as this and other embroidery stitches were often used to decorate crazy quilts. Here, the outer patches are generally linked with bright blue stitches, just as the innermost ones are stitched in red, but they give way here and there to white.

Whether the maker was influenced by crazy work or not, the general effect of the coloured stitching is to brighten up the rather plain everyday clothing fabrics used for the patches. Similarly, the random placement of occasional light patches, and also the mingling of tweedy patterns and textures, helps to keep the design alive.

The canvaswork panel is signed 'Mary Bowen' and although the picture could have been a self-portrait of Mary with her cow, it is more likely to have been copied from a child's colouring book.

Hand stitched and quilted wools and tweeds.
Welsh. Late 19th century. 173 × 145cm (68 × 57in).

◆ English Medallion ◆

This is a coverlet, not a quilted work, and it is probably the oldest piece in the book. Dating is always difficult because patchwork can include fabrics collected over a long period, even as long as a hundred years. Here, the birds probably belong to a chintz of about 1830, the blue pattern can be dated to about 1840, but the fabric with the black ground and full-blown roses suggests a much later, but still Victorian, period. As a design, the quilt is particularly striking in its use of interesting fabrics.

Central motif

The most popular method of setting out an English bedcover at the beginning of the 19th century was the 'framed' pattern, which involved a central motif or specially printed panel surrounded by many borders, usually all different. This example may have been started from a sample pack of printed furnishing cottons. It is structured around a medallion-type design, with a strong central image for which birds and flowers have been cut out of a printed material and appliquéd onto a separate fabric.

This technique is called *broderie perse* and was often applied over a quilt, the common practice being to cut carefully the printed flowers, birds and trees from a piece of printed chintz and re-arrange them in an artistically satisfying form. They were then sewn onto a foundation fabric. In this way a yard of expensive fabric could be spread over an entire bedcover and the images on the print became decorations in their own right.

Mosaic effect

Flowering trees were popularly created with this technique and sometimes embroidered embellishments were added. Here, only the central medallion has been given this treatment, so that it stands out and gives the whole quilt a focal point.

The quilt is made of pieced triangles and squares of various sizes. It is in fact something of a hodge podge, with patterns merging into one another to create an effect not unlike an Italian mosaic floor. The four diagonally set patches are very unusual.

The birds which appear in the central medallion are to be found in the body of the work, more humbly anonymous in their printed setting, and help to coordinate the whole design. The rather jumbled arrangement is redeemed by the choice of colours: the small curly print with its willow-pattern blue and white and the earthy, stony tones.

The sides and bottom border of the quilt have a rose-coloured band leaving the pillow end of the bed plain, so the piece was definitely designed for use and not just as a pretty decoration.

The whiteness of the backing in the central medallion draws the eye, throwing the appliquéd shapes into strong relief, and this is further accentuated by the patchwork frame with its black background.

Hand stitched and appliquéd chintz and cotton.
English. c 1850. 240 × 229cm (94 × 90in).

◆ Circus Star ◆

This exuberant quilt is an adaptation of a traditional star or sunburst pattern. It looks as though the maker had seen some quilts of this type and made her own interpretation, perhaps from memory. The indications are that the maker was Welsh – the quilt is thought to have been purchased originally in Wales, and the spiral quilting, and the pink squares and the rectangles at the edges, are typically Welsh. The backing fabric (not shown) dates from around 1875, so the quilt was probably made in about 1880. Differences of style in the making up, indicating that the quilt may have been sewn by two people, could also account for some of the design contradictions within this interesting piece of work.

Pattern problems

The maker has had to grapple with problems of shape and scale. She started with an eight-pointed star in red and enclosed this in a sort of octagon created by an outer ring of diamonds and stars.

Overall, the impact of the shapes is confused because so many odd elements have crept into the background, threatening to overpower the stars. One is very much aware of the scattered quality of the odd squares, triangles and half stars which have been contrived to link the diamonds. The device of adding two rows, each of five rectangles, to the top and bottom in order to elongate the design is unnecessarily clumsy, since the central star could have been completed at the top and bottom.

The corners have been consciously planned, with the four corner squares seen as isolated blocks rather than as an integral part of the design. The borders themselves show a greater confidence, with their good proportions and strong colours, and the quiltmaker or makers appear to have felt more at home with this part of the design.

Colour confidence

One of the best qualities of this quilt is its controlled use of colour. Although the deep pink squares round the sunburst sit rather oddly and are too dominant, the use of colour is largely successful. The clusters of red draw the eye and are quite dazzling against the cool blues. The paler patches impart a feeling of movement and of background light to a quilt which, in spite of its many drawbacks, has an unquenchable cheerfulness.

The red stars add to the exuberance of this design but nearly bring about its downfall by entailing innumerable odd-shaped filler patches: there is a lot to be said for keeping patterns simple.

Hand pieced and quilted cotton.
Welsh. c 1880. 226 × 204cm (89 × 80in).

◆Strippy & Plain Gold Quilt ◆

In Wales, as in the North of England, quilting has always been considered a craft in itself, not just an extension of patchwork. Plain fabrics that showed off the quilting patterns most clearly were preferred, either as whole cloth quilts or sewn in contrasting stripes in the strippy tradition.

The thickness of the layers and the texture of the filling affected the size of the stitching and the appearance of a pattern. Welsh quilts, usually filled with wool, were heavier than those where cotton wool or cotton wadding constituted the filling.

In poorer households, however, thrift might dictate the recycling of filling materials. Worn blankets were popular, although the thicker areas were difficult to quilt. In the poorest homes, old clothes were sometimes unpicked, pressed and laid out as flat as possible. Indeed, many a Welsh quilt that had seen better days itself became the padding for a new one.

The quilts on these pages demonstrate the quality of texture that results when wool-filled materials are quilted. Compared with the softer-looking cotton-filled quilts, like that on p55, the ridges produced by the lines of quilting are stiffer and more sculptured. The effect of working motifs reminiscent of the Celtic tradition in such thick, intractable materials recalls the strong textural relief of carved wood or weathered stone.

Red and gold strippy

This is a typical everyday quilt, sturdily constructed of closely woven sateen in a rich colour combination favoured by Welsh quilters in the early years of this century. The thorough and imaginative quilting of the strips shows popular patterns, including the round Snail Creep, large flat leaves (in the red strips) and (in the gold strips) Church Window.

Plain gold quilt

This quilt could almost be a carved wooden panel, golden with a patina of age. It conveys a sense of solidity: its weight on a bed must be warm and satisfying.

The sculptural effect is perhaps reinforced by the unusual configuration of the quilt's pattern elements. Such a square central motif would often be bordered by concentric bands of patterning, but here it is set into a series of parallel up-and-down runs of pattern, evidently worked in a sequence of strips as the quilt passed through the quilting frame. Spiral, half circle and half leaf shapes are the main motifs.

Plain gold quilt. Hand quilted cotton. Welsh. c 1930. 218 × 198cm (86 × 78in).

Red and gold strippy. Hand pieced and quilted cotton.
Welsh. c 1900. 208 × 198cm (82 × 78in).

◆ Molesworth Mon Amour ◆

In the past, quilts have often been used to commemorate some significant event or to express the political feelings of the day. Dinah Prentice is a modern quiltmaker who certainly uses her quilts politically, but to present a contemporary philosophy – that of peace. Even the titles of her works are seen as an important part of the whole, reinforcing the visual message, and the names are carefully chosen to make an impact.

At present she is closely involved in the fight against nuclear armaments, and the title of this quilt links the nuclear base at Molesworth, with Hiroshima, via its reference to the French feature film 'Hiroshima Mon Amour'.

Initially trained as a painter, Dinah Prentice is interested in lettering as a way of making statements which will have an impact. You might say that she uses her quilts as political banners. Although she employs traditional quiltmaking techniques, the political and intellectual content of her work really takes first place and cannot be ignored. She regards sewing as a purposeful thing, however, and very much enjoys the tactile pleasure which she gets from handling the textiles themselves – something that painting does not offer.

The quilt was made in homage to the women of the anti-nuclear protest movement. It expresses Dinah Prentice's hostility to any defence policy based on nuclear weapons. It is not the first quilt that she has made on this theme, and although it and parallel works are ostensibly a plea for peace, the imagery is sombre and uncomfortable, full of sharp, jagged, stabbing shapes and cold, arid colours: black and battleship greys on a white and desert-yellow background. The shapes reflect the small objects pinned by protesters to the high wire fencing which encircles the nuclear camps, the fencing itself being represented by the simple, straight-

lined grid which runs over the background yellow and white and behind the shapes.

Technique

Dinah Prentice begins by making several collages. Later, she makes paintings and drawings of the work and the final design is enlarged to its full size. This cartoon is then divided into several large areas, usually dictated by the straight lines. These areas are taken one by one and sub-cut into smaller pieces and eventually into templates.

The fabric patches are then cut and sewn together, working backwards in the reverse sequence used for cutting up the cartoon, the pieces fitting together in an angular jigsaw pattern. When one area is complete, she moves on to the next, until the entire cartoon has been dismantled.

A close-up of the quilt shows a hand-quilted grid design, unusual for Dinah Prentice who normally ties the layers together. Here, however, the quilting is an integral part of the design, representing the pattern made by the wire fence.

Machine stitched and quilted cottons and silks.
English. 1983. 256 × 212cm (101 × 83in) Dinah Prentice.

◆ Diamond in a Square ◆

The Diamond in a Square is a typical Amish design, being bold both in its concept of simple shapes with a strong focal point and in its use of colour. The central diamond is similar to the medallion type patterns characteristic of early English quilts.

Amish colours

Strongly contrasting colours were typical of the Pennsylvania German quiltmakers and particularly of the Amish. In no other part of America would such bold, large-scale colour contrasts have been used, with such a clear and unequivocal leaning towards colour rather than complicated design. The lack of patterned fabrics is also typical of this Swiss German religious sect: patterns were rejected as being too sophisticated and worldly.

Each of these quilts has the thin outer border in a contrast colour which is generally used to finish off the Diamond in a Square design. This particular pattern was generally made of wool in strong, positive colours, and it is the choice of these colours and their juxtaposition that creates the wonderful glowing effect.

Red Diamond in a Square

The demanding red of this quilt is contained within a cool green ground and framed by a dark blue border. The balance of the dominant red diamond and inner border at the centre gives the quilt a strong focal point.

A lightweight filling has been used. This was normal practice and allowed very fine and elaborate quilting patterns to be worked in small, even stitches. In this particular quilt, a circular feather pattern has been stitched in each corner square and meandering feather patterns are found in the blue borders and the narrower red inner border.

In the central diamond an eight-pointed star is outlined several times and surrounded with a circular feather design. The large expanse of green has been quilted more simply in a diamond filler pattern.

Blue Diamond in a Square

Here we can see what happens to an identical design when it is tackled by another quilter with a different colour sense.

The blue central diamond is much less forceful: blue is, after all, a receding colour compared with advancing red. There is also a less well-balanced use of colour in the border. The red corner squares, although similar in proportion to the corner squares in the other quilt, are much more dominant.

The fine quilting has a seven-pointed star in the centre, surrounded by small eight-pointed stars and then a circular feather pattern. Looped feathers appear in the large red corner squares and the borders.

Blue Diamond in a Square. Hand stitched and quilted wool and cotton. American. c 1900. 193 × 196cm (76 × 77in).

*Red Diamond in a Square. Hand stitched and quilted wool and broadcloth cotton.
American. 1915. 188×183cm (74×72in).*

•La Mer & Twilight•

Both the quilts on these pages were made by modern quiltmakers and both rely on the surface treatment to create their impact. Another similarity between these two quilts is the way in which they illustrate the freedom that modern designers feel to make quilts purely for decoration and not as warm bedcovers or for other practical purposes.

This is a comparatively new approach to quiltmaking. Admittedly the Victorians made their outrageous crazy quilts for show, but I do not see how these could be called works of art in the sense that the quilts made by contemporary artists can be rightly regarded as textile art. Only in the last fifteen or so years have many painters and designers turned to quiltmaking because it offers colour and shape as well as texture and form to the adventurous and exploratory artist.

In recent years, the challenge of manipulating a flat surface has been taken in various directions by different artists, but in these two quilts, more than in any of the others represented in this book, the fabric itself becomes part of the three-dimensional pattern.

La Mer

Phyllis Ross is inspired by the rhythms and order of the natural world, and it is not especially difficult to see the inspiration for this particular work, in which a series of ripples or wave-like patterns, in an all-over texture, are emphasized by highlights and shadows formed by the quilting technique which raises the cloth.

The ripple effect is created by Italian quilting, in which coloured wool yarn is threaded between two layers of fine white Habutai silk which have been stitched together to make narrow channels. This produces a soft, pliable fabric which holds its shape yet has a constantly mobile quality, endlessly fascinating to the eye.

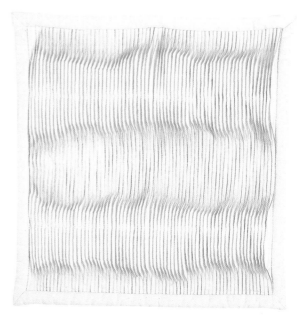

The bright yellows, magentas and cyan blue used for the stitching and the coloured wools threaded through the white silk channels produce ethereal colours of a delicate and subtle, yet almost startling, beauty.

Twilight

Eng Tow treats fabric as if she were making origami. Her pleats, with their changing directions and rippling surfaces, are like folded paper. This quilt is made of white polyester/cotton, pleated along its length, with satin stitches machined along the folded edges in many different colours. As in the previous quilt, the result is deceptively delicate; its strong yet subtle impact imparted by the textural, sculptural quality as well as the colour combinations. The result, as with Phyllis Ross's quilt, is a work of art to be seen and enjoyed rather than used.

'Twilight'. Hand pleated and machine stitched white cotton and sateen. English. 1978. 71 × 71cm (28 × 28in). Eng Tow.

'La Mer'. Machine stitched and quilted Habutai silk and fine cottons.
English. 1982. 172 × 160cm (68 × 63in). Phyllis Ross.

◆ Tree of Life ◆

This fine appliqué quilt belongs to a purely decorative quiltmaking tradition far removed from the pieced utility quilts of the settlers. It is the work of some leisured needlewoman with the time to create an object to embellish her home. She seems to have set about the project with the same self-conscious artistry that she might on another occasion have employed in her watercolours.

Indeed, the formalized character of the more elaborate flowers on this improbable plant suggest that the maker was drawing on some specific reference for her inspiration: perhaps a needlework pattern book. The stylized pomegranate, buds and blossoms are classic shapes familiar from embroideries and popular in printed textile designs.

Design inspiration

The Tree of Life, Tree of Paradise or Flowering Tree is a design as abundant in its symbolism as in the variety of its fruit and flowers. Originating in India, it became one of many stylized forms to be adopted by the West, and to be reinterpreted by 17th- and 18th-century Indian manufacturers commis-

sioned to print fabrics for the growing European and American markets. Images of the tree, reflected back and forth between East and West, inspired new designs with each technological advance and stylistic development in the textile arts. Individual motifs from these fabrics are found in *broderie perse* (see pp 78–9).

But to trace the sources of inspiration is by no means to diminish the quiltmaker's achievement. The firm lines, strong shapes and satisfying curves suggest a confident needlewoman, well used to working with figurative motifs and able to assemble them as naturalistically as the stylized forms permit. The detailing of tendrils in stem stitch extends the fluid lines of the organic shapes.

What the fabrics tell

Seventeen different plain fabrics have been used in a fresh and delicate combination on a white ground. When new, the contrasts must have been brighter, almost garish. The maker must have chosen colours with as much care as she would select her skeins of yarn for a piece of needlepoint, and she had at her disposal almost as wide a range of artificial dye shades. Only the brown of the trunk shows signs of fading unevenly, the worn ridges further emphasizing the texture deliberately added by embroidery. Was this brown an unreliable dye, or an older fabric? Have other colours in the quilt already decayed more than this and been restored? The blue and mauve petals look like replacements, as is the new green binding along the top edge. The pinks have faded and mellowed more uniformly with age. Such hints, together with the 'flattened' feel of the quilt overall, show that this quilt was used as well as admired.

Detail of the central area showing the fine stitching of the appliquéd flowers, leaves and stems.

Hand stitched and quilted cotton with cotton wadding.
American. c 1920 218 × 183cm (86 × 72in).

◆ North Country Plain Quilt ◆

This quilt is a typical example of the meticulously detailed yet flowing work that has brought Amy Emms so much acclaim over the years. Now in her eighties, she was taught the traditional techniques and particular patterns of North of England quilting by her mother.

Quilting tradition

In the North of England, in Durham and Northumberland in particular, there is a long tradition of quilting. It is seen as the most valued part of a bedcover; the patchwork takes second place and is often used as the underside of the work – a point of view frequently shared by the Welsh.

As in America, quiltmaking became less popular in northern England at the beginning of this century but experienced a revival in the 1920s. In the mining areas, widows, or the wives of men injured in accidents, used to run quilting clubs to help subsidize their household. If a number of customers could be persuaded to order a quilt each, a club would be started and the members would pay the quilter a regular sum until all the quilts had been made and paid for. Each quilt took about three weeks to make and the work was poorly paid.

Those whose husbands were in work might join one of the church quilting clubs, which made quilts to raise money for less fortunate families or for the local church. When a quilt was finished, each person brought along food for a celebratory 'faith tea', trusting that, like the miracle of the loaves and fishes, there would be enough to go round. A new member would be low in the pecking order and given the boring jobs – starting with the threading of needles and progressing to sewing a simple pattern. She would only be allowed to take her place on the quilting frame after a long and thorough apprenticeship.

North Country patterns

This superbly quilted work demonstrates Mrs Emms' remarkable skills and displays a number of traditional North Country patterns. The centre consists of eight pairs of scissors and the border is of small roses, combining running feather and lined twist. She has put curled feathers in each corner and arranged among these are several leaf-type patterns. The rest of the filler pattern consists of a tiny diamond grid. The completed work has a soft-yet-firm textural quality, which is one of the most pleasing aspects of plain quilts. Mrs Emms has used a deep blue cotton that contrasts well with the white on the reverse side, and she has finished the edge with piping.

The combination of many different quilting patterns into a coherent whole demonstrates a mastery of quilt design as well as advanced sewing skills.

Hand quilted cotton and chintz with polyester wadding.
English. 1982. 147 × 109cm (58 × 43in). Amy Emms.

◆ Clean Getaway ◆

It was not until 1980, after working as a calligrapher, graphic artist, mapmaker and weaver, that Linda MacDonald decided to concentrate on quiltmaking. She is primarily concerned in her quilts with the illusion of space and the establishment of three-dimensional shapes and planes within that space. Instead of making a flat pattern, she has extended the use of the repeated forms so that they make fascinating, multi-directional images within a unified whole, in which the eye is led in and out of the various and diverse design elements, and in opposing directions. Tension is thus created through contradiction.

Her work explores similar themes to those used by Pauline Burbidge, but whereas the latter's work is disciplined, Linda MacDonald creates a less restrained world of science fiction and fantasy.

Three dimensional effects

In this machine pieced, hand appliquéd and hand quilted cotton quilt, Linda MacDonald gives free rein to her interest in creating illusions of space and three dimensions. The flat plane is destroyed by suggestions of

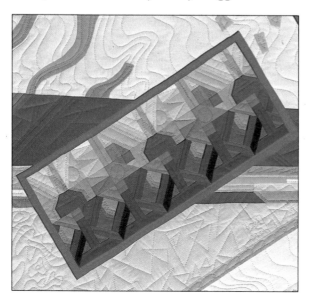

different levels and directions to give a chaotic impression of forces beyond control.

The design has been very carefully and meticulously worked out beforehand, reflecting her graphics and map making background. The surfaces reach out in all directions, pushing out beyond the confining edges of the quilt. There is a feeling of vast spaces, but within the rigid framework of strong, direct geometric lines are softer, more nebulous, almost organic shapes.

The hand quilting is an important and integral part of this quilt, used to reinforce the three-dimensional quality of the work: patterns change from plane to plane, helping to carry the eye through the design – an effect heightened by the colour theme.

Restrained colours

As if to compensate for this bombardment of shape, movement and linear patterning, the colour range is almost monochromatic. Linda MacDonald exploits the tonal range of the chosen colours to suggest space as well as the enormous differences in direction and scale of the various components. In fact the contrast between the rather intimidating, strange, science fiction quality of her work and the warmth of the colours adds interest to this complicated piece.

Here we can see a whole spectrum of reds ranging from the dark, indeed almost black, mulberry to palest rose pink, with many muted rather smoky pinks in between. Dotted about you can find a number of patches of luminous sky blue – not very noticeable but adding an important element to the atmosphere of the whole.

Smaller, denser patches set within a narrow border, echoing the border round the quilt itself, stand out against the larger background shapes. The more you look into a good quilt, the more your curiosity is rewarded by intriguing details and new images.

Machine stitched, hand appliqúed and quilted cotton fabrics.
American. 1983. 237.×208cm (92×82in).
Linda MacDonald

*Pauline Burbidge checking colour patches against her
drawing for 'Pyramid in Disguise' (see pp 60–1)*

2. DESIGNING

To develop a personal, intuitive sensitivity towards design is an important element in successful quiltmaking, but it helps to be aware of basic design theories. This knowledge need not be rigidly applied but it enlarges visual awareness and points to the ways in which particular effects may be achieved.

There is no easy answer to the question: 'How can I design better quilts?' The skill has to be built up over a period of time, and as you become more experienced you will gain the confidence to take short cuts.

Most quiltmakers start off by making traditional style quilts: this serves as an apprenticeship, familiarizing them with the various sewing techniques and the different fabric effects before they move on to more innovative designs. These can be pictorial or abstract geometric images but the most successful quilts have usually been developed from a specific theme. Pauline Burbidge, for example, has devoted her attention to creating an illusion of space within a quilt.

This chapter starts with the basics of quilt patterns which will be of interest to beginners. A quilt presents a visual mixture of tone, colour, fabric and patterns, and all these interacting elements are considered individually, like layers to be gradually peeled away, revealing what lies underneath. In most cases, this is a basic underlying grid, and there are many suggestions as to ways in which this can be altered to produce more exciting and unusual designs.

The chapter ends with the work of five contemporary designers. Each shows a serious and long-term commitment to quiltmaking, extending the tradition and creating new directions for future growth. Some of them like to know exactly what their work is going to be like and start off by making many designs on graph paper. Others prefer to have more freedom. Michael James, for example, suggests that his strip piecing method allows greater spontaneity in design.

You must choose whatever method suits you best: the aim of this chapter is simply to demonstrate certain design theories which may take you some way towards achieving your goal. Although you cannot hope to create a masterpiece with every quilt you make, it is worth developing new ideas to produce a quilt that is fresh and original, rather than one which simply repeats an already overworked formula.

TYPES OF DESIGN

The principles of basic design are interrelated, but, for clarity and simplicity, tonal contrasts, space, perspective and colour are treated as separate subjects and are discussed more fully later in this chapter. It is, however, best to ignore colour initially, and begin designing in black, white and intermediate shades of grey. This will enable you to concentrate on the overall shape of the design without the distraction of colour.

ONE-PATCH DESIGNS

If you are designing a quilt for the first time, one-patch patterns are a good place to start. They are among the most basic types of quilt design, but can be used to make dramatic and effective patterns, for example Sunshine and Shadows and Trip Around the World.

One-patch patterns consist of a single shape – usually a square, rectangle, hexagon, triangle or diamond – repeated all over the surface of the quilt to create a mosaic effect, the pattern being created by changes in tone and colour. Each of the common single-patch shapes has its own character: squares give a solid, static feel to a design; triangles have a strong diagonal movement; hexagons are static, intricate, decorative shapes, while diamonds are elegant and lively, especially when used to make star patterns with their strong radial symmetry.

Bear this in mind before you start cutting out patches: patterns need not be centred and regular, but if they are to be successful they must be thought out, even though the finished quilt may at first glance appear to be very simple. One of the least successful forms of quiltmaking is that based on the honeycomb pattern. It requires enormous effort and energy in making up the hexagon patches, but lacks overall design impact. Time spent planning a design will ensure a successful effect and will also speed the sewing process.

To make a one-patch design, start by making an outline, drawing a scaled-down version of the finished quilt size. Divide this into squares, triangles, or whatever your choice of patches. Do not make the patches too small and fiddly, unless your quilt is to be an endurance test rather than a design masterpiece.

SQUARES
If your design is to have a central square, it is essential to have an odd number of rows each way, so that there will be an even number of rows on each side of the square. Use square graph paper as a grid.

SQUARES

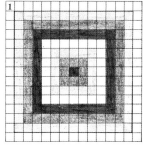

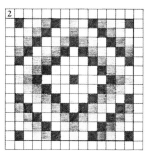
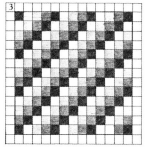

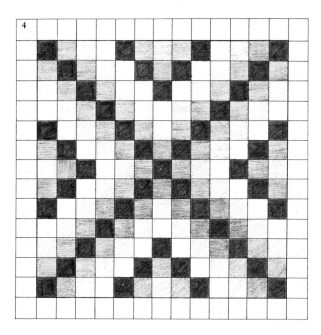

1 *The concentric squares emphasize the centred design. The effect is four-square and stable but rather static.*

2 *Here the shading creates an expanded diamond shape which instantly has more movement and tension than the previous one, which simply reinforces the square.*

3 *A square one-patch quilt can easily be given a strong diagonal movement, breaking away from the static image.*

4 *The area is divided diagonally into quarters and the eye is pulled away from the centre and out to the corners.*

RIGHT-ANGLED TRIANGLES

EQUILATERAL TRIANGLES

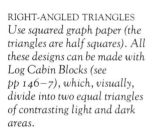

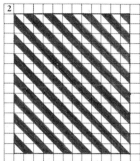

DIAMONDS

RIGHT-ANGLED TRIANGLES
Use squared graph paper (the triangles are half squares). All these designs can be made with Log Cabin Blocks (see pp 146–7), which, visually, divide into two equal triangles of contrasting light and dark areas.

1 *Radiating diamonds*
2 *Diagonal lines*
3 *Diamond outlines*
4 *Chequerboard*
5 *Zigzag*

The advantage which all these triangular designs have over patterns made with squares is that you can achieve a more even, unstepped diagonal flow, increasing the sense of movement and direction.

EQUILATERAL TRIANGLES
Isometric graph paper consists of equilateral triangles, and provides an instant grid for shapes based on single or multiple triangular units. Two equilateral triangles form a wide diamond, while six make a hexagon.

DIAMONDS
These are the basic shapes used for many one-patch patterns, including Tumbling Blocks and stars. A wide diamond is used for Tumbling Blocks (see p104) and six-pointed stars, and is based on an isometric grid; a narrow diamond must be drawn (see p134).

Diamonds joined into stars are the most strongly radiating of all patterns. They have a strong focal centre while tonal contrast in the patches stimulates optical vibrations. The eye is constantly attracted inwards only to be drawn out to the edges – the points of the star – and back to the centre, an effect easily emphasized with tone and colour.

HEXAGONS

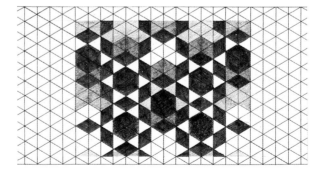

HEXAGONS
Most people think instantly of hexagons as soon as one-patch patterns are mentioned. Unfortunately, most hexagon quilts are traditional in the worst sense: it is much more interesting to break away from the rosettes which so often cover a quilt's surface indiscriminately and create a more complex design, maybe even adding linking patches – diamonds and triangles. Hexagons must be drawn on isometric graph paper.*

99

BLOCK DESIGNS

In block designs, the surface is divided into a number of repeated units, which are usually square and measure from 20 to 37cm (8 to 15in) across. The individual blocks are made up of a number of patches of different shapes. Within this framework lies an infinitely varied scope for design, which has provided inspiration for a long line of quiltmakers stretching from the pioneering American settlers up to present-day quilters like Pauline Burbidge and Michael James, featured later in this chapter. The reason for this is that when a number of blocks are joined together, totally new overall images can emerge,

so that the design of the individual blocks is submerged in the pattern of the whole.

This last point is the basis of making a block design: it is vital to see what several blocks will look like when put together. The block patterns that look most attractive in isolation are by no means the ones that will look best in a full-scale quilt. Often, the reason that they look attractive is that they are symmetrical and are visually complete in themselves, but they produce static and boring designs when repeated. An asymmetrical block which looks unfinished and unbalanced, on the other hand, has the potential to produce a fascinating and unpredictable pattern when it is repeated over the whole quilt.

SYMMETRICAL BLOCKS
These have a balanced arrangement of shape, tone and colour distribution. In essence, the design is static, especially when the blocks are set straight; a diagonal setting introduces more movement.

by alternating pieced blocks with plain squares. These are also useful devices for drawing together a design formed from a collection of totally different blocks as are found, for example, in an Album quilt.

1 *In the Dresden Plate block, the image is complete in itself and does not touch the sides of the square at any point. This means that when blocks are set together, the overall pattern consists of a series of isolated images. This effect can be achieved with any type of block by adding lattice strips or*

2 *The Missouri Star block is formed from four identical quarters. In this type of block the eye does not move across the design, though this can change when the block is repeated and new patterns link the blocks.*

2

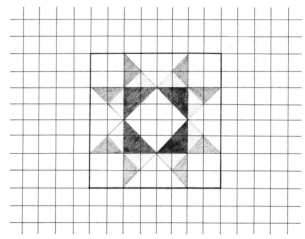

SYMMETRICAL BLOCKS **1**

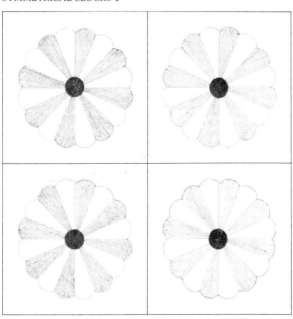

2 repeat

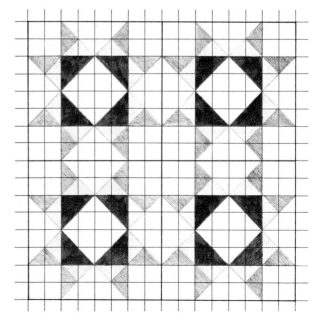

3 In this Storm at Sea block, the gradual turn of the line produces the illusion of a curve with a sense of movement that overcomes the static quality of the block's straight lines.

3

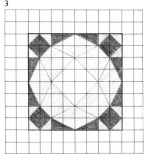

4 If a block is diagonally symmetrical, as in the Bull's Eye pattern, the arrangement is inherently less static. Contrast and pattern-making potential can be considerably increased if the corners at either end of the diagonal division are not identical.

ASYMMETRICAL BLOCKS
Asymmetrical designs present more of a challenge to the quiltmaker and offer the possibility of creating livelier and more interesting statements. They are naturally more active, keeping the eye moving round the pattern. This activity may be intensified by strong contrasts of shape, tone and colour. When the blocks are joined together they create an uneven, illogical pattern, setting up areas of tension. The blocks can be placed randomly on any of their four sides to increase the irregularity, or positioned to make symmetrical patterns. Changing colour from block to block further exaggerates the irregularity of the overall pattern. This can be gradual or there can be dramatic changes from block to block.

1 Asymmetrical blocks with a directional bias can be arranged in expanding star shapes, in diamonds or zigzags, or positioned in such a way that they create strong diagonal emphasis. The jagged shapes on this block are based on cut paper.

2 Asymmetry can be created by distributing the familiar patchwork shapes in a deliberately unbalanced way, so that the visual weight of the block is uneven, and a group of blocks builds up a strong rhythmic pattern.

3 repeat

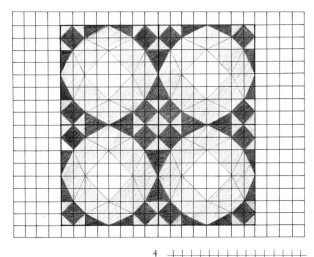

4

4 repeat

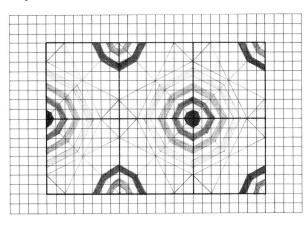

ASYMMETRICAL BLOCKS **1**

2

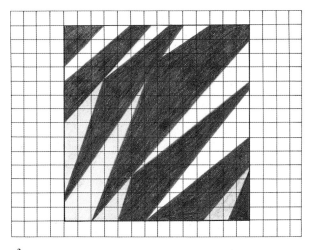

FRAMES AND BORDERS

Most antique quilts have borders, often quite deep ones, which provided the opportunity for elaborate quilting. Many contemporary quilt artists, on the other hand, carry their designs right up to the edge and use only a narrow finishing strip to surround the design.

Borders can be used to frame a design and emphasize its symmetry or to give visual relief to a complicated pattern. These factors should be considered at the design stage: borders added as an afterthought tend either to dominate a design or are so weak that they exercise a negative effect.

Appliqué (see pp 148–53) borders can be designed by cutting paper strips as long as the borders, folding them and cutting out linked shapes.

REPEATED BLOCK BORDERS

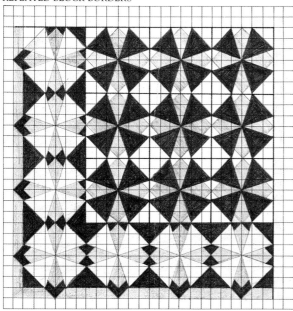

SWAG BORDERS

CENTRE POINTS AND CORNERS

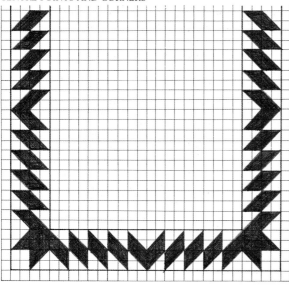

REPEATED BLOCK BORDERS
The tone and colour combination may be the same as in the main design, but used in different proportions, perhaps, as here. The outer kaleidoscope blocks also extend into the edging strip.

CENTRE POINTS AND CORNERS
Whatever type of border is used, make sure that it flows round the quilt evenly, especially at the corners. If there is a strong movement in one direction, the image must be reversed at the centre point and at the corners to give a balanced design. Corners should be designed as separate but linking squares.

SWAG BORDERS
This swag border, made by the folding paper method, echoes the theme of the tulips in the main block and shows a fine adjustment, giving a smooth turn to the corner. If your quilt is to be square, it is easy to organize an even number of repeats all round, but if you have a rectangular design, it frequently happens that you can fit ten repeats down the sides, say, but only seven and a half at the top and bottom. In this case, one way to make the border pattern fit is to design a separate image for the centre of each border which can be finely adjusted to take up more or less space as desired.

MEDALLION QUILTS

Medallion designs consist of a series of borders, formed from repeated blocks or shapes, which lead the eye to the centre of the quilt. When planning a design of this kind, always start at the centre with a large, strong image and then work outwards, adding successive borders that both echo and complement the central image without diminishing its impact. Medallions are more visually satisfying if they are based on squares rather than rectangles, with the elements designed as multiples of a single square grid.

AMISH DESIGNS

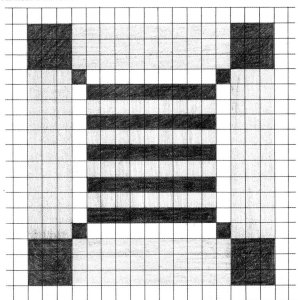

MEDALLION STARS

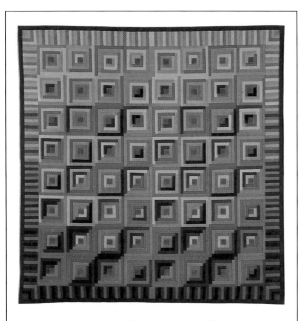

MEDALLION STARS
The central area of a medallion pattern must be strong enough to act as a focal point, and many old quilts use a star as the central image. Here, any tendency which the larger star might have to radiate outwards, taking the eye away from the centre of the quilt, is counteracted by the smaller central star.

Varying the size of the patches used in successive borders provides a contrast of scale while still allowing the large central motif to retain its full impact, particularly if the border patches echo elements of the main image and are cut from darker and less strongly contrasting fabrics.

AMISH DESIGNS
The medallion quilts for which the Amish are best known contrast completely with the elaborate patterns found on English medallion quilts of the late 17th and early 18th centuries. Amish quilts reduce medallion patterns to barest essentials – just a strong central image surrounded by a single border – and the result is both dramatic and elegant, the visual impact coming from a bold, sure use of colour and scale, enhanced by the elaborate quilting patterns.

This Log Cabin quilt by Susan Carr started broadly as an exercise in complementary colours: red (light-toned diagonal stripes) and green (dark-toned stripes). It is divided vertically into two identical halves, each with a vertical and a horizontal colour shift. The horizontal shift is fairly straightforward, but the vertical shift is much more complicated and involves swapping the eight colours in the top row for the eight in the bottom row in sequence. This system fulfils the object of creating a subtle change in tone from top to bottom within a set scheme. The border is simply designed as a frame, using only the green half of the Log Cabin squares, and echoing the light to dark movement which characterizes the rest of the quilt, rather like a shadow passing over its surface.

TONAL CONTRASTS

Although at the back of your mind you will already be developing ideas about the colour themes you will use, it is much easier to discover the full design potential of a pattern if you restrict yourself initially to working with tonal contrasts of black, white and shades of grey.

Tone represents the degree of lightness or darkness of a colour, with black and white forming the strongest contrast. Varying tones can be used to define shapes and create patterns, but can also create an illusion of space and volume and give a three-dimensional quality to a flat surface. In this way, tone is closely linked to space and perspective, both of which are discussed more fully overleaf.

If you are in any doubt about how to represent fabric colours as tone, looking through half-closed eyes (or even photocopying your colour references) will help you to analyse tonal values and will heighten the relationship between light and dark ones.

LOG CABIN VARIATION

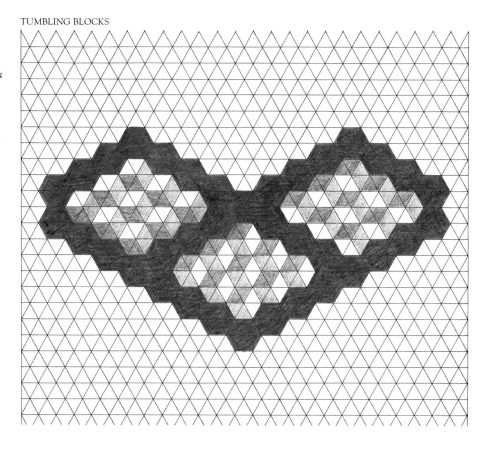

LOG CABIN VARIATION
The Log Cabin pattern (see p 146) offers great scope for manipulating tone, with the block divided diagonally into a light and a dark half. The tones can be graded to create an illusion of space, and this effect is intensified if the movement from light to dark is combined with a reduction in the width of the strips.

TUMBLING BLOCKS
The Tumbling Blocks pattern is formed from groups of three wide diamonds, each in a different tone. It is an example of the way in which tone can be used to suggest how a three-dimensional solid would be illuminated by a light source. The basic design shows the light coming from one direction only, but the pattern immediately becomes more complex if several different light sources are implied.

TUMBLING BLOCKS

FIGURE GROUND REVERSAL

Patterns based on equal proportions of black and white or two contrasting colours produce an even tension across the surface. The extremes of contrast and perfect balance between the black and white shapes make it difficult to focus on either. Confusion as to which is the background colour and which the foreground is known as figure ground reversal.

TONAL EXPERIMENTS

In general, light shapes seem more buoyant than darker ones. Too stark a contrast creates a very harsh visual effect. Breaking up the shapes with line and intermediate tones creates a gentler effect and can give the effect of three-dimensional relief. There are no fixed rules as to whether light or dark shapes will recede or advance, but darker shapes stand out on a white ground, and on a dark ground the reverse happens.

FIGURE GROUND REVERSAL

TONAL EXPERIMENTS

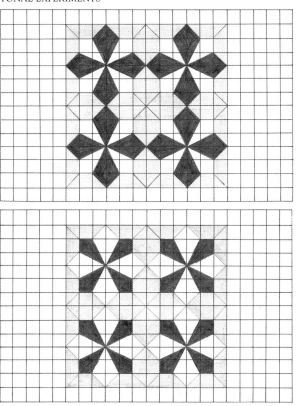

In 'Blue Undercurrents' by Michael James, shown in colour on p65, there is a constant movement of tonal contrasts. Comparing a black and white photograph with a colour reproduction of the same quilt is an informative tonal exercise in which the colour is translated into precise tones of black, grey and white (a photocopy gives the same effect, but the subtlety is lost).

MOVEMENT AND SPACE

The illusion of the third dimension is an aspect of quilt design which fascinated quiltmakers in the last century and still continues to intrigue contemporary quilt artists. The flat plane is seen as a challenge and introducing an illusion of space and volume has been a motivating force behind the designs of, for example, Pauline Burbidge and Linda MacDonald. Each has a unique approach, inviting you to see the world through the window of her quilt.

Patchwork patterns distort the flat plane in a number of ways. The simplest examples, the traditional Tumbling Block and Attic Window, use diagonals to suggest volume and depth respectively. The Card Trick block, with its use of overlapping shapes, implies that one plane lies behind the other. Tone and colour further exaggerate the spatial effect: warm colours come forward and seem heavier; cool colours recede into the background and are lightweight.

Gradation emphasizes all these effects: a slow change in direction, shape, size, tone/colour or pattern makes the most convincing impact.

CHANGING THE BASIC GRID

The simplest type of pattern making is the repetition of a single shape or image, and this is the principal method used in patchwork design. In the basic grid, the horizontal and vertical lines intersect at regularly spaced intervals, producing a repeat pattern of shapes – usually squares, rectangles or triangles – of a uniform size. When the proportion or the direction of the grid is changed, the intrinsic balance is destroyed and new shapes emerge to contrast with one another. The more gradual the change, the more effective it is as the shapes seem slowly to advance or recede into the distance.

Remember that a grid provides a linear pattern for the quilting stitches on a whole fabric quilt as well as the outlines for a patchwork design. The individual grid shapes may be made up of single pieces of fabric or with a series of appropriately distorted block repeats. In the more irregular grids a different template is needed for each fabric shape. Either make a full size plan or calculate the size of each patch from a fairly large scale drawing.

GRID PATTERNS

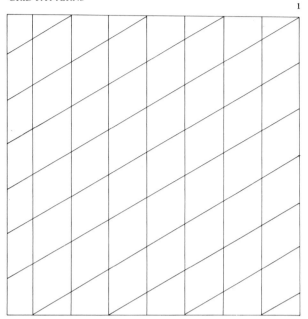

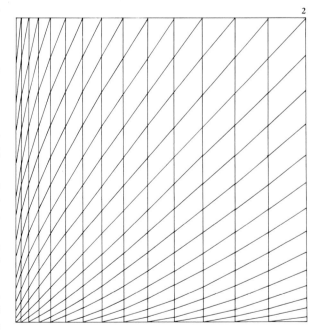

1 *A simple diamond grid is drawn on isometric graph paper.*

2 *Changes in both direction and proportion make shapes diminish towards one corner.*

3 *Grid lines are closer together at the edges of the square. Gradated tone could suggest a domed surface with the light, perhaps, shining down on its centre. The four quarters are identical.*

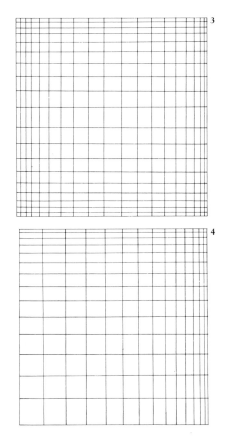

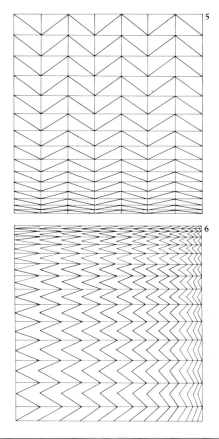

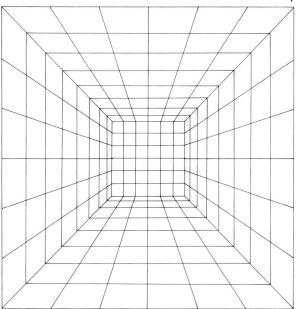

4 A scaled-up quarter section of grid **3** decreases in shape and size towards one corner.

5 The rectangular grid is disected by diagonal lines to form decreasing chevrons.

6 Diagonals transform grid **4** into a series of zigzags.

7 Four planes seen from a one-point perspective create the illusion of a four-sided box shape.

Linear patterns and solid forms in 'Shooting Gallery' by Linda MacDonald (1983) display a bizarre range of graphic devices used to distort the perspective and to convey an impression of motion.

CHANGING THE BASIC BLOCK

Changing the basic shape of your block is a simple way of altering a traditional pattern to create new images. Various ways of doing this include: repeating blocks as a half-drop, instead of setting them side by side; using only a proportion of the block, so that individual blocks merge into one another; and varying the block in two different sizes, superimposing one over the other. With each of these methods, the proportions of the basic block remain the same, but you can also change the proportions within the block.

Altering the block by condensing it into an increasingly narrow rectangle, for example, means you can use it in a graded grid (see pp 106−7). This change retains the right angles, but you can also change the block to an irregular four-sided shape. Choose fairly simple blocks, without pronounced diagonals, like Ohio Star.

HALF DROP
Here, Churn Dash blocks are arranged in a half-drop pattern instead of in straight rows. In addition, they are interlinked, to form a more concentrated design, in which the blocks are no longer seen as isolated units.

COMBINING SIZES
This Pinwheel variation shows a small-scale block superimposed upon a large one, creating a secondary grid-like pattern. This could be combined with a contrast in tone between the large and small blocks to suggest space.

OHIO STAR VARIATIONS
The Ohio Star is a nine-patch square block, but the square can be changed to a rectangle, or the block can be redrawn with new proportions. Further distortions can be made by superimposing the block on a graded grid.

OHIO STAR VARIATIONS

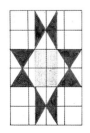
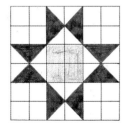
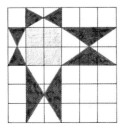

HALF DROP

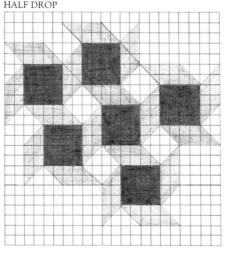

COMBINING SIZES

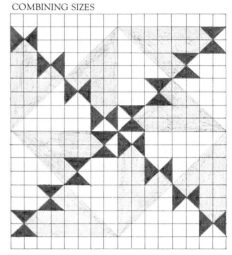

CROW'S FOOT VARIATION

REFLECTIVE IMAGES

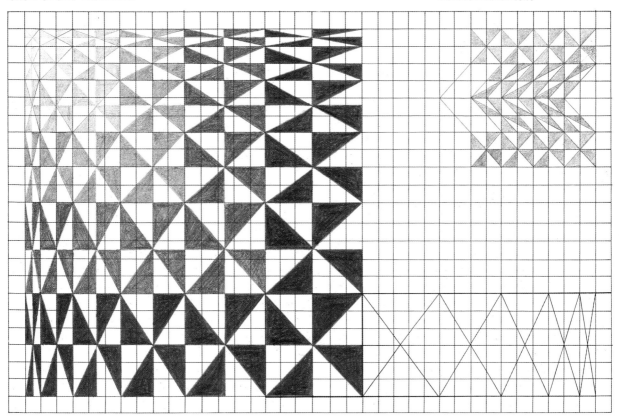

CROW'S FOOT VARIATION
Instead of keeping to square Crow's Foot blocks, the size and proportions of each block are altered to fit a graded grid, with tone added to emphasize the change.

REFLECTIVE IMAGES
Here, reflective blocks sandwiched between straight rows give the feeling of a sudden change in direction.

GRADED REFLECTIONS
The previous idea can be extended to produce an image which is at the same time reflective and graded.

GRADED REFLECTIONS

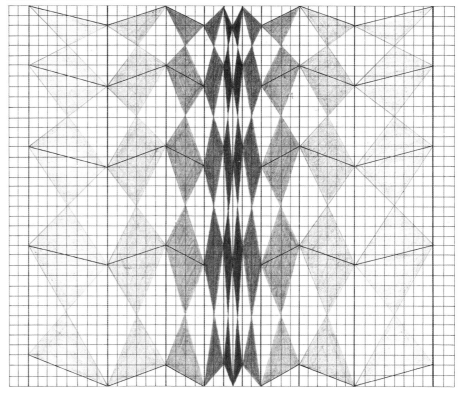

ONE-POINT PERSPECTIVE

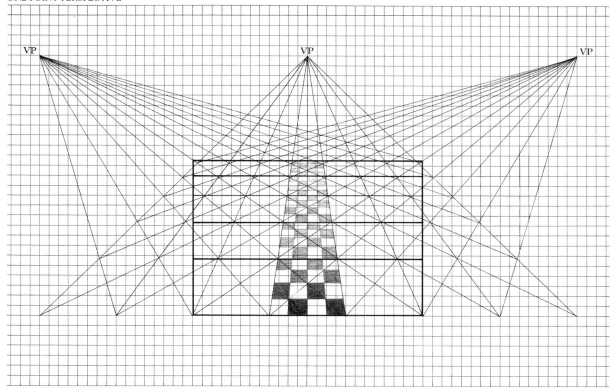

PERSPECTIVE

Drawing in perspective on a flat surface – a sheet of paper or a quilt top – creates the illusion of receding space, or the impression of a three-dimensional object with depth and solidity. Contemporary quiltmakers often explore its abstract capacity to make exciting visual statements as well as optical paradoxes that contradict the limitations of the quilt's flat plane.

Perspective devices give a variety of grids on which patchwork designs can be based. One-point perspective is perhaps best epitomized by the image of straight railway tracks converging at a vanishing point on the horizon directly ahead, with the horizontal sleepers growing visually closer together the farther away they are. Two-point perspective will show three sides of a solid, hence the illusion of volume and depth.

The technicalities of perspective touched on here are a starting point for design. It is not necessary to follow the rules too rigorously to give an impression of receding distance or relative volume in a quilt surface. Remember, though, that if you wish to superimpose a block repeat on to a perspective grid, all the elements of the block need to be in the same perspective.

One of the joys of perspective is to use it paradoxically, by establishing one perspective and including elements from another plane, as in 'Shooting Gallery' on p 107.

When designing from perspective, draw up a larger area than you will use, and then choose a square or rectangular section of the drawing, depending on your quilt shape. You may want to use the network of lines that establish the perspective themselves as part of the design, or to superimpose extra shapes on or between them. You may want to home in on one area and expand it to fill the outline of your quilt.

With these perspective designs, and indeed with any of the non-traditional/irregular patterns shown on the preceding pages, first sketch your ideas on a small scale, and then make an accurate final drawing about three times larger.

ONE-POINT PERSPECTIVE
Lines from points equally spaced along a horizontal base line converge on a vanishing point VP *at the centre of the 'horizon' line.*

To establish the position of intermediate horizontals, which need to grow closer together as they approach the horizon, *add two secondary* VPs *on either side of the main one, and at an equal distance, and connect the points marked on the base line with each of these* VPs. *Where the new criss-cross grid lines intersect, draw the extra horizontal lines. Further subdivisions can be worked into the basic grid.*

TWO-POINT PERSPECTIVE

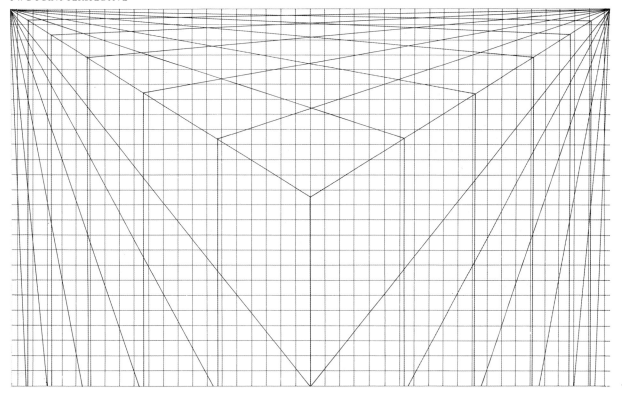

TWO-POINT DESIGNS

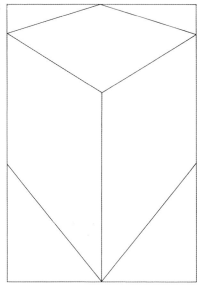

ADDING PATTERN

TWO-POINT PERSPECTIVE
In two-point perspective, lines converging towards two separate vanishing points delineate a cube, which is seen from an oblique angle revealing the top and two sides. If the vanishing points are lowered, the angle will be less acute, but the area of the top will be correspondingly diminished.

The vanishing points might be altered to an asymmetrical relationship, so that the cube appears to be off-centre. An irregularly shaped solid could be depicted, or the 'closed' box could be made to seem open sided, or even transparent.

TWO-POINT DESIGNS
Cubes made in two-point perspective can be squared off and used as a single image, repeated or integrated into a larger overall design.

ADDING PATTERN
Add patterning in the same perspective. To subdivide the sides, begin by drawing two diagonals to find the centre point. Run a line through this towards the vanishing point to maintain the perspective. Keep the vertical line parallel with the sides of the figure.

COLOUR

So far in this chapter we have been working in terms of tone, and concentrating on the formal aspects of pattern making. Now we discover the rainbow, as it were, and look at effects of colour. It is worth setting aside for the moment your own personal likes and dislikes. Build up a full colour range of fabrics as your quiltmaking palette, and experiment with them as you would with a well-stocked box of paints. Tonal exercises, using lighter and darker versions of the basic hues, will help you achieve exciting and lively combinations of contrasts, the opposite of the monotony of a scheme based on the same tonal values.

Colours, however, may each evoke complex emotional and even physiological responses, and add a powerful dimension to tonal exercises. Red is vibrant and strong: a relatively small amount is eye-catching. Yellow is lively, the brightest of the primary hues. Blue appears cool and calming. Colours have associations with temperature, and can appear to affect space and dimension. Warm yellows, oranges and reds are active and come forward, while cooler mauves, blues and greens, especially when pale, convey an illusion of space. They also seem more passive. Monochrome designs, using tones of one colour, can suggest spatial effects but lack the richness of multi-coloured and tonally complex combinations.

Colours are never completely isolated, of course. They are always seen against a background, and when two colours are juxtaposed each influences our perception of the other. Combinations of larger numbers of colours provoke different reactions. Brilliant, multi-coloured designs stimulate the eye with many flashing shapes; others produce a subdued effect with subtle gradations of tones, perhaps limited to a 'family' of colours from a segment of the spectrum. Study the colour schemes in the gallery quilts for inspiration.

THE COLOUR WHEEL

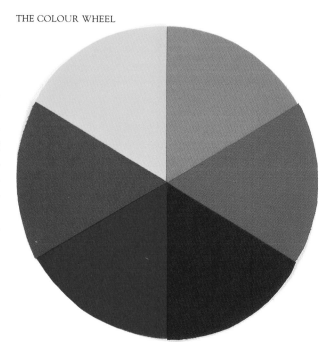

THE COLOUR WHEEL
This device is a useful tool for showing some basic colour relationships. Red, yellow and blue are the primary hues, from which all other colours and tones are derived. Orange (red plus yellow), green (yellow plus blue) and violet (blue plus red) are the secondary colours.

The stylized wheel shows colours in separate segments: in the rainbow or prism each colour blends into its neighbour, with an infinite number of gradations, say, of violet and purplish tones, between blue and red.

Harmonious colour combinations are those which have some pigment in common. They are simply found as adjacent colours on the wheel.

Colours which have no pigment in common are said to contrast. The most extreme contrasts are those between complementaries – pairs of colours diametrically opposite on the wheel, eg red/green.

BACKGROUND CONTRASTS

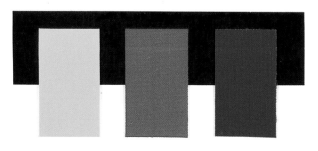

BACKGROUND CONTRASTS
Designs using the three primary colours are strong and festive, with each colour struggling to dominate the others. The background exercises a dramatic influence: against white, both yellow and *red appear darker and duller. So does blue, but it also gains in depth. Against black, the primaries glow and have an inner strength, becoming sophisticated. Yellow is brilliant, red glows and blue is luminous, as in Amish quilts.*

TONAL VALUES

TONAL VALUES
Every pure colour has a potentially infinite progression of tones from light to dark – comparable to all the gradations of grey between white and black. A red might go from lightest pink through medium tones of rose and crimson to dark dusky wine. Generally, the lighter colours are called tints and are associated with luminosity and with lightness in weight. Darker gradations are known as shades, and suggest shadow and, sometimes, solidity.

Putting these colours in tonal sequence gives the eye a gradual transition, blurring shapes and suggesting dimensional space. Juxtaposing them out of their gradated sequence gives a more abrupt transition, whose contrast makes shapes stand out clearly from one another.

The presence of these tints and shades can neutralize the strong contrasts of primary and secondary colours.

COMPLEMENTARY CONTRASTS
The pairs of complementary colours are judged to balance optically in different proportions. However, colour composition demands something more interesting than simple equilibrium.

1 *Yellow and violet balance at a ratio of one to four. The wide visual gap between these light and dark colours is muted when tints and shades of the hues are present.*

2 *Red and green are said to be tonally similar and to balance in equal amounts. Distort these proportions and the smaller amount of red becomes increasingly active.*

3 *Blue and orange balance equally at a ratio of three to two. Mixing these pigments (as if with paints) produces intermediate tones which have an affinity with both and act as a bridge between them.*

COMPLEMENTARY CONTRASTS

WORKING WITH FABRICS

People respond very positively to quilts, perhaps because they can combine the three-dimensional and tactile qualities of the fabrics that are so familiar to us – the very texture of our everyday lives – with the aesthetic stimulus of an exciting design statement.

The colours in a quilt as opposed to other art forms are expressed through the medium of fabrics and dyes. The textural properties of the fibres, and the way they are woven, fundamentally affect the colour quality that we perceive. Cotton is opaque, light-absorbent and gives a solid colour. Wool's softer, more textured surface is also light-absorbent and matt, but has a greater depth of colour. Silks and satins are light-reflective or luminous, depending on their weave; with different coloured warp and weft they become iridescent. Velvet and corduroy reflect and absorb light according to the direction of the pile: the richest black is that of velvet.

The best way to study and observe the potential of the various fabrics to express a design is to handle as many as possible. Experiment to see how they respond to folding, pleating, wadding – all the relief effects you may want to use in a quilt. Collect samples of the different fabrics in one colour to make a more vivid comparison.

When I teach quiltmaking classes, the students' choice of fabrics and colour schemes for the quilts they plan at first almost invariably reflects the clothes they wear. In order for a design's potential to be fully realized, however, you may have to incorporate colours you would not normally have thought of using: some bright complementary focal point to set off a moody area of muted tones, for example, or a patterned fabric to texture a particular shape or area.

Make a wide-ranging fabric collection, something between a colour palette and a scrap-bag. Above all, avoid buying sets of ready-assorted fabrics for patchwork, a practice equivalent to painting by numbers.

Arrange your collection of scraps and swatches colourwise, following the spectral wheel, and then grade the light, medium and darker tones of the colours. If you are in any doubt about the tonal quality of a patterned fabric, half close your eyes to eliminate some of the pattern.

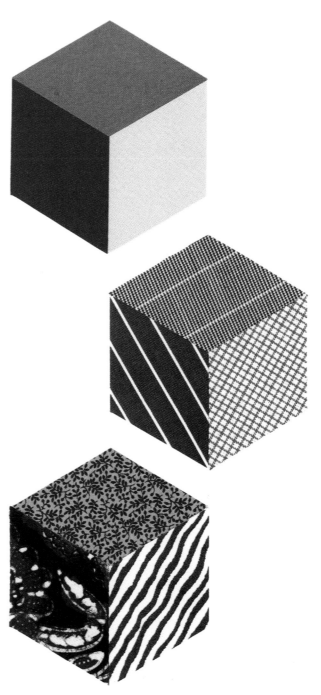

THREE TUMBLING BLOCKS
The top one shows plain fabrics in light, medium and dark tones; the middle block uses printed fabrics to give a feeling of texture and, because of the stripes, direction. The bottom one uses prints which have been chosen to break up the solid outline of the block, creating a more abstract pattern.

DYEING FABRICS

If you fail to find just the right colour, try dyeing your fabrics. Pauline Burbidge and Susan Carr, for example, use dyes to control the subtle gradations of tones that their designs require. Cold water reactive dyes are best and natural fibres such as wool, cotton and silk are the most receptive.

One way of unifying an assortment of fabrics in different patterns and colours is to dye them a single colour. Cottons take on deeper shades than mixtures containing man made fibres, and this unevenness can be used to add depth and interest to a harmonious range.

PATTERNED FABRICS

Whether you use plain or patterned fabrics or a combination of both is a matter of personal design choice. The main thing is for every fabric to contribute towards enhancing the whole effect. Some quiltmakers prefer the simplicity of plain fabrics, which have no blurring effect on the outline of the patch and can thus make the boldest, most dramatic statements. Others feel that patterning adds a richness implying texture, which can elaborate the underlying design.

It is a mistake to try slavishly to imitate the use of pattern in old quilts by using modern fabrics. The subtlety we admire in these old textiles is so often due to the fading, mellowing properties of the old dye-stuffs and natural fibres. Even when today's textile manufacturers revive the old prints, they can seem brash and crude. Worse still, they are sometimes so recognizable that they act like labels, signalling the shop that the fabrics came from rather than the design of the quilt.

Representational patterns Beware of allover repeats of flowers and motifs that have too strong an identity to submerge into pattern and so call too much attention to themselves. Organic forms are acceptable when they are so small or so muted that they become abstractions. They then have an anonymous quality and can replace plain/solid colours, contributing the impression of mottled texture or relief in 'background areas'.

Geometric patterns Spots, stripes and checks have a timeless abstract quality that enables them to be used as 'texture'. The directional use of stripes can help articulate a pattern, suggesting a

sense of movement, or establishing different planes within a surface.

Bold patterns Surprisingly, perhaps, the large swirling shapes of paisley patterns, exotic batik prints and large-scale representational patterns can be useful when they are 'dismembered' into separate pieces for patchwork shapes, and when they contribute abstract shapes to give movement and life to the design.

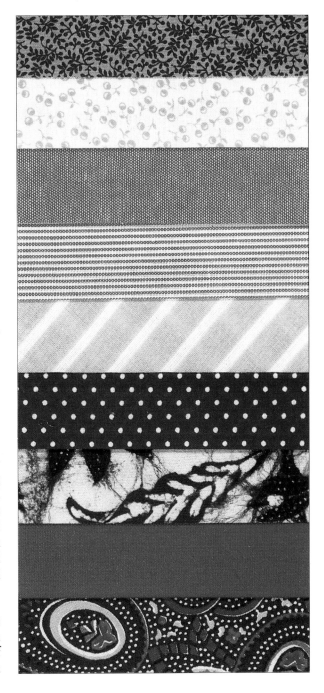

MAKING
A DESIGN

The process of designing a quilt is a highly individual one, and every quiltmaker eventually develops a particular way of working. Below is a demonstration of a design process using coloured pencils, graph paper and photocopying. The design is based on a nine-patch block called Jacob's Ladder, and I began by drawing a series of blocks set together in fours to see what patterns would emerge when the blocks were placed and coloured in different ways. After experimenting with one pattern and rejecting it, I selected a zigzag pattern, developed from block B (below), which seemed to offer more potential.

The next stage was to draw a repeat of seven by seven blocks with a hard lead pencil on tracing paper placed over graph paper, to give an under-

lying grid. I made several photocopies and then after some experiments with tonal and colour contrasts, I used red and green pencils (complementary colours) to make a series of designs. The theme which eventually began to emerge involved increasing the proportion and shapes of one colour and decreasing the other.

The red/green design is at an early stage, and I am still considering several factors. I prefer to let the pattern run to the edge, avoiding the rigidity imposed by a frame, but I might possibly decide to add a red/brown binding to set the quilt away from the wall. The red/green contrast makes a dynamic visual impact, but tonal or textural variations in the colours of the actual fabrics used should add interest.

BASIC BLOCK

FOUR-BLOCK REPEATS

A

B

C

SIXTEEN-BLOCK REPEAT OF A

BASIC BLOCK
The single Jacob's Ladder block has a diagonal bias which can be quarter-turned to make closed symmetrical repeats or an open pattern.

FOUR-BLOCK REPEATS
Three examples from my series of four-block tonal sketches give an immediate impression of A symmetry, B directional
movement, and C strong diagonal bias.

SIXTEEN-BLOCK REPEAT OF A
The more blocks you put together, the more an overall pattern emerges. Block A, at first a strong, stable shape, becomes too rigid and wallpaper-like when repeated over a large area.

TRACING PAPER REPEAT OF BLOCK **B**

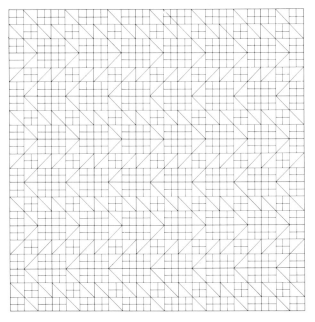

COLOURED DESIGN **2**

COLOURED DESIGN **1**

COLOURED DESIGN **3**

TRACING PAPER REPEAT
OF BLOCK **B**
*When you start to experiment
with designs to the scale of the
finished quilt, bear in mind
that the patches should not be
so small that the design will be
laborious to make up. If, on
the other hand, the block is too
big, the finished design may
resemble a flag, with little
room for contrast. A*

*reasonable size for the Jacob's
Ladder block would be
21 × 21cm (8 × 8in), so the
finished quilt would measure
147 × 147cm (56 × 56in),
plus any borders: this uses 49
blocks, sufficient to make an
interesting effect on a
workable scale. The design
here is developed from Block **B**
(opposite).*

COLOURED DESIGNS
*The design which I prefer – at
least so far, though I might
experiment still further – starts
with red at one end and
gradually gives way to green.
I like the shattered image
effect, as well as the way in
which a completed block
emerges from time to time.*

*The tonal gradations
resulting from the sketchy*

*effects of rapid colouring in
pencil give an interesting
variation of depth. I might
capitalize on this accidental
effect with dyes of different
strengths, altering the reds and
greens tonally towards brighter
or muddier shades.*

*Alternatively, an element of
pattern in the fabric might be
used to achieve an equivalent
richness.*

CONTEMPORARY QUILTMAKERS

This chapter is devoted to an exposition of some of the work and design ideas of five contemporary quiltmakers, each with a highly individual and dedicated approach, and who have given the art a new dimension. I find their work an inspiration. They have each described in their own words how they went about producing the quilts shown on the following pages.

THE ILLUSION OF SPACE

PAULINE BURBIDGE trained and worked in fashion design, making her first quilts while freelance pattern-cutting. A full-time quiltmaker since 1979, she exhibits and teaches on both sides of the Atlantic. Each individual work, which involves the manipulation of extremely complex patterns, is the result of experimenting with many variations of a design before she arrives at the final one.

'I have always been fascinated by the use of pattern: the way in which a single unit changes when repeated over a larger area and dramatically different patterns are created if the units are rearranged. This is what first attracted me to patchwork, but I also like the straight seams and geometric shapes. The medium is ideal for me.

I started by making several quilts to traditional patterns. This gave me a basic understanding of quiltmaking. I then decided to work with pictorial images, reducing them down to straight-line designs for easier piecing. Butterflies, birds and fruit baskets were favourite themes. Eventually,

STRIPY STEP **1**

2

3

4

STRIPY STEP

1 When I design a quilt, the first stage is to make design drawings on graph paper, defining the design and the repeated block. This is then worked in tone – black, white and grey – to sort out tonal values and shapes.

2 A single block is enlarged to the final size and coloured in with pencil or painted. An identical line drawing is made later, to be cut up and used to make templates.

3 The next stage is to make designs showing colour variations. In the case of this particular quilt I made several variations on the design of the top left corner before I was satisfied.

4 The border, as in many of my quilts, is a continuation of the outside blocks, extending the overall design. When the design is finished, I select the fabrics, grading them according to tone and choosing colours that go well together.

pictorial quilts were no longer a challenge. I felt that I was working to a predictable formula, so I decided to create a new set of problems to solve, concentrating on geometric patterns with an illusion of depth. Traditional quilts had always been a great source of inspiration to me, and I next became intrigued by those patterns that suggested three dimensions, such as Tumbling Blocks and Log Cabin. I particularly enjoyed manipulating such blocks to make original images and this new direction made me completely reconsider my approach to quilt design.

I began to simplify my design ideas to the basic essentials and produced a number of small pieces using the Log Cabin block which eventually led to 'Cubic Log Cabin' (see p 7). Later ideas began with cardboard models placed in front of mirrors, the subsequent designs being worked out on isometric and perspective graph paper.

I have purposely departed from the symmetry of traditional quilts to create designs which are asymmetrical, often flowing diagonally across the quilt. I am especially interested in breaking up patterns in order to create new ones and in using tone and colour to change the identity of each block. Normally, my designs are worked out on graph paper with coloured pencils.

The design of 'Stripy Step' was fairly typical of the way in which I work. The idea was to form solid three-dimensional shapes which would then disintegrate and change into areas of stripes and flat pattern. The shapes evolved from previous quilts and from designs on isometric graph paper.

In general, I now prefer to work on large-scale quilts. Each one can take from two weeks to two months to design and another two or three months to make.'

PYRAMID IN DISGUISE

CIRCULAR SERIES **1**

2

3

PYRAMID IN DISGUISE
This design was created in a similar way to 'Stripy Step'. The areas of crazy patchwork were pieced spontaneously, though the tones and colours were carefully chosen, the idea being to create a mass of crazy patchwork merging into solid shapes of plain cloth.
The back of 'Pyramid in Disguise' was also pieced – a new departure for me – the crazy and plain areas lying in opposite corners to their position on the front of the quilt (see also pp60 – 1).

CIRCULAR SERIES
Another series of quilt designs was drawn and planned on circular perspective paper.

1 *As usual, the first stage is to make pencil drawings on the quarter-circle graph paper to define the shapes and the blocks.*

2 *The coloured sketch uses tonal variations typical of the Tumbling Block.*

3 *The finished quilt is in soft rich colours of Hunan silks.*

DESIGNING A WHOLE CLOTH QUILT

DEIRDRE AMSDEN, who studied illustration at the Cambridge School of Art in England, has been making quilts since 1976. She was a founder member and first president of the Quilters' Guild. She is equally at home with abstract or pictorial quilt designs, but has recently turned her attention to quilting as a creative art in its own right, concentrating chiefly on expanding its textural qualities. Here she describes the ideas behind the design of one such quilt.

'Many quiltmakers still refer to North Country, Welsh or American patterns taken from old quilts, and if they design their own pattern it is usually of a traditional kind. I began looking for patterns made by everyday objects, consolidating ideas which I'd had in mind for some time. One winter was very cold, with heavy snowfalls, and I noticed the patterns made by shoes, dogs, cats, birds, cars and cycles.

I took photographs of, for example, the way in which a cycle tyre crossing a footprint obliterates part of the latter. Optimistically, I thought that if people could be persuaded to walk across a large sheet of paper, my quilt would be designed! One afternoon I set a large sheet of white newsprint outside my house, together with a sheet of foam rubber soaked in grey (water-based) paint, and asked passers-by if they would make the necessary footprints, but somehow it did not work out. The paint was too thin and men walked across the paper in one stride, but it did give me a clearer idea of how to tackle the design and get better patterns.

Back in the studio, I made the paint thicker and darker and took more prints, this time from my family and friends and the cat. Rubbings were made from car and cycle tyres. Next came the tracings and the photocopies, then the final design and templates.

I then had to experiment with different types of fabric. The final design was to be hand quilted, using a large frame, though the experimental pieces were held in a hoop. I wanted to try different fabrics, thicknesses of wadding and threads, and also work out how best to mark the fabric, white being especially difficult. After completing the sample in white satin acetate shown on the opposite page I felt pleased and excited by the design, but eventually decided to use a fine pure silk or Viyella for the piece itself. It was important to find a white fabric which had a

TRACINGS

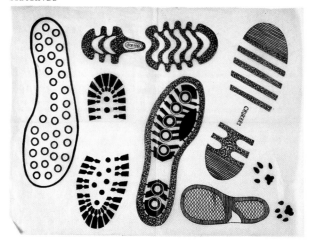

Once I had a reasonable collection of patterns, I traced them all out on tracing paper with a black felt tip pen, then made photocopies of each. Right and left feet were obtained by copying both sides of the paper. Tyre patterns were made as repeated units, so only a very small section, giving one complete pattern repeat, was needed.

TEMPLATES

A template was made for each print by sticking a photocopy to thin card and cutting out either the black or the white shape. Some shapes, such as circles, needed interconnecting bars to prevent the central portion from dropping out. Very intricate patterns were left as solid areas to be drawn directly on the fabric.

Repeat patterns for tyre marks had to be completely accurate so that the repeat sections would fit together and make a continuous track.

blue-tinted reflection rather than a yellowish tone. This cool quality could be emphasized by lighting the finished quilt with a blue light.

I feel that there is no need for a border and I like the way the footprints walk off the quilt. The edges will be folded in and hand stitched.'

FULL-SCALE DESIGN

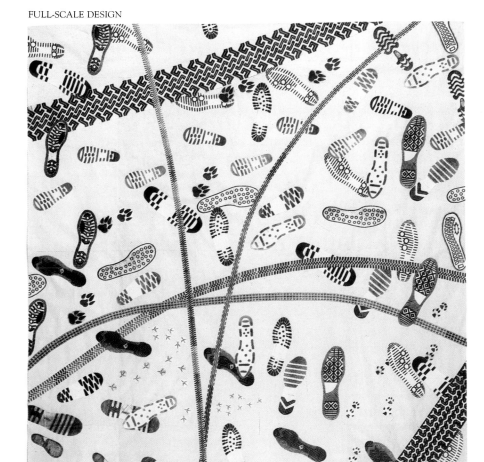

FULL-SCALE DESIGN
A large sheet of paper, the finished size of the quilt (2.5 × 2m/96 × 76in), was laid on the floor and the cut-out photocopies were arranged on top. It was important to get varying lengths of stride, so I walked barefoot across the paper and stuck the prints down accordingly.

SATIN ACETATE SAMPLE
After initial experiments, I decided to use white satin acetate, 100g (4oz) wadding and silver thread, hoping to recreate the sparkling effect of snow with these materials.

I marked out the design with a blue pencil, but discovered that this fabric needed much lighter pressure than would be required for marking cotton or Viyella, and the marks remained visible after quilting.

During quilting, it became obvious that the tyre pattern was too intricate and would look muddled, and that the shoe patterns were too literal and needed to be freer. Fine details were being lost because of the thick wadding.

VIYELLA SAMPLE
Viyella finally seemed a more snowy fabric than satin. Marking is still a problem: I might place the quilt top over the original design so that this shows through, and outline the shapes lightly with a grey coloured pencil.

SATIN ACETATE SAMPLE

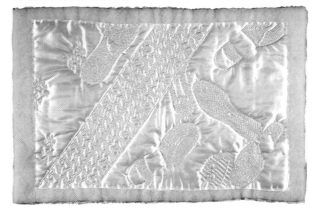

VIYELLA SAMPLE

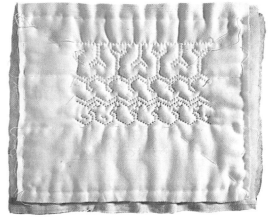

ABSTRACT IMAGERY

DINAH PRENTICE first studied painting at the Royal Academy Schools in the late 1950s, and was a co-founder of the Icon Gallery, Birmingham, England. She has been making quilts since the mid-1970s, and exhibited in Quilt National, Ohio, in 1983 and 1985. Her work has a quite different motivation, design process and form from other quiltmakers represented. It is firmly set, however, in the tradition of using powerful graphic forms to make forceful design statements. She explains how she moved away from painting and sculpture and began making quilted pieces.

'I discovered a new direction when I started to work using geometric forms generated from written marks. I liked the idea that all lettering comes originally from squares, circles and triangles and that, although these have been distorted by time and use into modern script, it is possible to convey so much experience by these shorthand forms and at speed. I liked the picture that the printed page made: all ticks and marks. I was fascinated by the relationship between print, word and image and developed my own language which I exploited in small sculptures and paintings. Ten years later and still working on the same theme, I had to patch some canvas together to make a whole piece and saw the possibility of sewing round the individual forms themselves instead of patching the canvas and painting the image across the patches.

I made some patchwork, first for the family and then for a wider circle. The quilts were large and I enjoyed the softness and lack of frame or stretcher. I wad, quilt or tie my present works for durability; they are as tough and portable as the functional quilts that I made for the family as bedcovers. Now, however, it is the subject that I want to deal with which is the springboard for the work, and I choose and arrange the materials and methods in order to achieve that end.

My earlier works were made from photocopies of collages scaled up to full-sized cartoons, but I later decided that it was better to make some drawings and paintings before I got so far ahead that I forgot the train of thought that had led to each work. This note-taking process itself led to some changes.

There is a belief that mechanical means can achieve the same results as the 'hand-made', better and faster. My belief is that the form or end result is not the same, and that carried in the time-consuming work of quiltmaking is a sublime and priceless commitment to ideas. Large sewn works are very seductive: they contain within themselves this great density and effort, but I wanted to be sure that the formal ideas contained in the work were at least as viable as the techniques, so all the work I have done since spring 1983 has been carried out in the form of paintings first and done as quilts afterwards.

My works are becoming more like landscapes. I need the escarpment of the sewn edge across the picture plane. New work will attempt to keep that and the flexibility of unstretched work while allowing for the freedom to paint. Where I shall go in the future I do not think about. I just work from idea to idea. What gets me out of my chair is not affection for form, mood or colour, but a fury with contemporary language and its underlying judgments.'

A4

This was the first definitive work, made after three years of traditional quiltmaking. The paintings I had sewn together in the early 1970s were too generalized in form and I had put them on one side, but they haunted me. I wanted to harness my ability to work densely on a large scale in the quilts to the more abstract and emotive ideas that had been in the earlier works.

I drew a large-scale cartoon of 'A4' and looked at it for a few days. I evolved the technique of sub-cutting the shapes (described in more detail on p84) in order to sew the shapes together.

A4

SIENNA STONES

MOLESWORTH MON AMOUR

The first small painting for 'Molesworth Mon Amour' (shown in colour on pp84–5) was made before 'Sienna Stones' but the quilt itself came later. At first, the gouache I worked on was in relatively bright colours (right), but gradually the memory of a newspaper photograph came back to me, and the prevailing greyness of the printed image affected the colours in a later design (below right).

MOLESWORTH MON AMOUR

SIENNA STONES

I work from collages which are themselves from papers that I have collected for subconscious reasons. Collages allow a certain degree of freedom or accident to influence the design. 'Sienna Stones' had been a companion piece to 'A4', translating into soft material the aesthetics of the printed page, but other works got in the way. I knew that my ideas were changing so fast that it would never get done if I did not put aside a couple of months at this stage.

The quilt was made after a dyeing course. I tried cold water dyes in 'Sienna Stones', but found some of the colour unsatisfactory. I was making a new discovery, although I was slow to realize what it was. I pinned the finished sewn face to the studio floor and sprayed it to tighten it; when it was taut like a canvas, I painted over the unsatisfactory colour in acrylic, as can be seen and felt on the bottom three feet.

My new discovery was that I wanted to paint the colour and to sew the canvas.

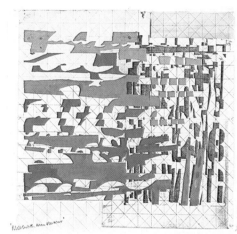

HERMENEUTICS

HERMENEUTICS

This was another emotional reponse to the proposed missile base at Molesworth. The colours of the finished quilt show the red breaking down under the force of the menacing black shapes, with small areas of white piercing through to the surface of the quilt.

COLOUR STRIP PIECING

MICHAEL JAMES studied painting and printmaking and has conducted workshops and lectured on quilt design in the United States and Europe. His work is included in public and private collections. His quilts display an absolute clarity of design based on a strong and intuitive colour sense and tightly controlled workmanship. Although the strip technique used is a relatively simple one, Michael James uses it in a most exacting and sophisticated way.

'One of the things that first attracted me to quiltmaking was the sequential constructive process by which quilts are built. I find this approach works well for me because it allows for a sort of give-and-take between me and the work. I can exercise a certain amount of control as the process unfolds, but the work itself determines to a certain degree what happens along the way.

A dozen years ago, when I first started making quilts, all my designs were first worked out on graph paper, usually with coloured pencils, which enabled me to work out the design problems. The resulting quilts were generally fairly strict interpretations of these preliminaries.

After some time I began to feel that this slavish allegiance to sketches eliminated any chance of spontaneity in the making of the quilts. I began to use drawings or maquettes only as occasional jumping-off points, creating a series of works in which the quilts themselves, rather than sketches, generated each successive work. This has allowed me greater freedom in my experiments with colour as well as with modular design units.

This development coincided with my first involvements with strip piecing. The construction method allows me greater spontaneity because it can be less predictable in its results and because the speed with which it can be carried out promotes experiment.

What follows is the way in which I might approach a new series of quilts destined for exhibition or retail sale.

Weeks 1 to 2 I start by choosing fabrics from my collection and making strip-pieced panels. I select colours in sequences that appeal to me; rarely for any specific reasons, but usually because I like them together. If I have specific templates and measurements in mind, I will cut the strips to correspond. If not, the strip widths are based on previous work which I found

A good sewing machine and a large table on which the work can be laid out in a logical sequence and where everything is to hand are both essential for modern strip patchwork.

interesting. Arranging the strips in the sequence in which they were selected and sewing them into panels is the most tedious aspect of the work, and depending on the number of panels required, can take up to three weeks to complete.

Weeks 3 to 4 I begin the actual designing in fabric, assuming I have prepared templates that will produce a particular type of image (curved triangular templates, for example, to create a pattern with movement, rhythm and a sinuous line, or angular, straight-edged templates for sharper, more rigidly geometric images).

I mark and cut the pieced fabric and pin each shape as it is cut to the pinboard on my studio wall. The relationships between the shapes begin to suggest how the overall design will develop, and I work with these relationships, standing back each time a new piece goes up and evaluating its influence on the rest, and at the same time calculating what might go where in the next selection. Eventually the overall image seems to reach its natural perimeters, sometimes dictating the creation of a border pattern to complement the main modular configuration. When not working on commission (when I must generally aim for a specific size), my quilts range from about 130cm (48in) square up to 220cm (80in).

Weeks 5 to 8 I may have completed a pieced top and begun its quilting. At this point I usually begin a second and even a third top, alternating between these and the quilting of the first.

With luck, I may have completed three new works by the twelfth week (pieced and quilted), but in practice I rarely manage to complete more than six average-sized quilts in a year.'

THE SIXTH EXERCISE **1**

THE SIXTH EXERCISE **2**

THE SIXTH EXERCISE
This was made to the design of the maquette shown below. The work consists of two panels of machine pieced and quilted cotton, with polyester wadding, each panel measuring 130 × 175cm (48 × 66in), commissioned by the Barstow School, Kansas City, Missouri, for their new library. This piece was the first in which I worked with the particular configuration of wide and narrow strips of cloth in alternation, and eventually led to the making of seven quilts using that same wide/narrow configuration.

RHYTHM/COLOUR: SPANISH DANCE
Strip panels and maquette for a work which has been commissioned by the Newark Museum, Newark, New Jersey. The finished work will measure about 240cm (92in) square and about 10 panels will be needed. These are now finished: each panel is made up of 30 strips of coloured cotton and silk and measures 137 × 185cm (54 × 72in). In addition to the commission, there should be enough material to allow me to complete one or two smaller works.

SPANISH DANCE: PANELS

MAQUETTE IN PROGRESS

SPANISH DANCE: MAQUETTE

MAQUETTE IN PROGRESS
If I am working to commission, a preliminary maquette is usually required. I start by choosing the fabrics and making up multi-coloured panels, then painting paper strips to match. I use small-scale templates to cut shapes from the paper strips and glue these in place, usually within a simple square grid.

WORKING TO COMMISSION

LUCY GOFFIN studied ceramics but now makes quilts to commission and has exhibited in Great Britain and abroad. She also designs embroidery for Jean Muir and is a lecturer in textiles. Lucy Goffin's description of entering a competition and producing a work to commission is a good example of how a professional quiltmaker works. In particular, a lot of effort must go into the preparation and presentation of designs, so that the client has a clear idea of how the finished product will look. Every detail must be thought through from the outset, including payment terms and delivery dates.

'My brief was to provide a double-sided screen for a recently built library. The front of the building consists of three large glazed archways; the screen was to occupy the middle arch. On the outside, the screen had to be attractive by day and to allow the interior lighting to show through at night. From the inside, it had to provide privacy and act as a light filter to enhance the atmosphere. It also had to be designed to enable the windows to be cleaned with ease. The fabrics had to be cleanable and resistant to fire and fading as well as compatible with the tinted glass within the arches of the façade.

One reason why I was particularly interested in submitting ideas for this competition was that I had recently completed a similar but smaller project for a contemporary house and wanted an opportunity to design on a larger scale. It was an open competition and I was one of four people short-listed to submit design proposals.

My submission was as detailed as I could make it and contained several sections: first the main design, which was, in the event, the commissioned one, formed from four banners, measuring in total 3.7 × 2.4m (12 × 8ft), then came rough ideas for alternative schemes. I included photographs of the surrounding area which had inspired the patchwork design, and a thick file of fabric samples. Some of these samples consisted of swatches of the fabrics which I intended to use (these were mainly furnishing fabrics in a wide range of textures), others showed the types of quilting and the varied sewing techniques with which the patches forming the screen would be decorated. I described how the patchwork would be machine sewn.

Turning the design into reality proved quite a challenge as there were practical problems to overcome. In particular, it was important that the screen should hang correctly and the patches remain crisp and flat. I began by lining each patch, but as they were double sided and mostly made from heavy furnishing fabrics, this made them too bulky. Eventually, after I had enlarged the design to the finished size on graph paper, I made a backing template (finished size) from iron-on interfacing for each shape. This gave the patches body and kept them firm without adding bulk.

The intricacy of the patches themselves and the complications of hanging them separately made the actual construction time-consuming: overall it took four months to complete. I had never worked on so large a scale, and it was very encouraging to have the commission well received and to see the screen hanging in place.

THE DESIGN PROPOSAL

THE DESIGN PROPOSAL
The main design proposal, which was accepted: a screen of geometrically shaped, pieced fabrics, hanging in four long banners, all double sided and each measuring 3.7m × 60cm (12 × 2ft). Each banner is divided into panels with loops attached at the top and bottom. Lengths of aluminium (chosen because it is lightweight but strong, and I liked the contrast of metal with fabrics) would be slotted through the loops to connect the panels and enable the banners to be louvred to one side so that the windows could be cleaned. The design included spaces to allow light to pass through.

FABRICS

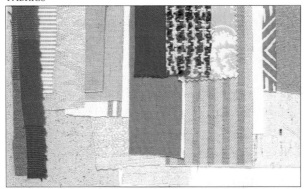

WORK IN PROGRESS
The patches all had 9mm (⅜in) seam allowances. They were cut individually, the interfacing templates were applied, and they were sewn into rows which were then joined into larger units. Working on such a large scale had its problems, but as each area was completed, I attached it to a pinboard in my studio so that I could view it from a distance.

I pleated some fabrics and in some cases pleats were already worked in the fabric. The light-reflective qualities of the fabrics form another important element of the design. The centre has been cut out of some patches and others pivot round on fine aluminium rods so that views can be seen through the screen, giving it another dimension.

FABRICS
Samples taken from the file of fabrics submitted with the design. The colours of the fabrics were chosen in sympathy with the building and to give tonal and textural contrasts within the design.

THE PATCHES
The shapes are basically the same on each side, but they vary tonally and use different fabrics. Texture is important:

VIEW FROM THE OUTSIDE
The screen was designed to be viewed from the outside as well as from within the library. Its colours and shapes echo those of the surrounding buildings.

WORK IN PROGRESS

VIEW FROM THE OUTSIDE

THE PATCHES

The author sewing together the blocks to complete the last in a series of quilts based on designs made from cut paper shapes.

3. SEWING

There is an infinite number of ways of sewing pieces of fabric together. This chapter introduces the principal techniques for patchwork or pieced work, where fabric shapes are joined to make various allover patterns, and explains the principles of appliqué, where pieces or layers of fabric are superimposed on a background. Both produce the 'top', which may be wadded and quilted – see next chapter – or simply finished with a backing, to produce, technically, a coverlet.

In patchwork, design and method are inextricably linked. Broadly speaking, the more complicated geometric patterns of diamonds and hexagons need the backing-paper method. Squares, rectangles and right-angled triangles all need ordinary straight seams, which you can sew by hand or by machine.

This chapter explains the preliminaries: the choice of fabrics and the process of making appropriate templates. It then illustrates in detail the techniques and tips for each of the different sewing methods, the actual process of joining the elements together, whether patches into blocks or blocks into larger units. A variety of appliqué techniques are tackled next. The final stages of assembling a top are common to both patchwork and appliqué: the appropriate sequence of sewing together the strips or blocks of patches and of incorporating any lattice strips or borders that your design calls for, and finishing off with edgings and backings.

Many people sew patchwork and appliqué by hand, convinced that hand sewing is intrinsically superior, perhaps because it takes so much longer. This is a mistake: some of the finest old quilts are those made to patterns devised by the early American settlers because they were quick and easy to sew. The choice of method should depend on your preferences. Hand sewing is a sociable type of work, which can be picked up at odd moments and carried around, whereas machine sewing requires a specific work area and can be more solitary. Machine work, on the other hand, produces stronger seams and is better for heavy fabrics.

Ideally, experimenting with samples will help you decide which type of work you prefer as well as that which best expresses your design. Hand appliqué looks very different from machine work, but though the difference is less marked with patchwork, hand sewn seams produce a softer effect, while the strong lines of machined work complement abstract designs.

GENERAL SEWING EQUIPMENT

Tape measure and metre rule or yardstick
Both are useful for measuring, and the rule can be used for marking straight lines.

Dressmaker's ruler This is a transparent plastic ruler, sometimes T-shaped, and printed with a square grid, used for adding seam allowances.

Coloured pencils These are much better for marking fabric than dressmaker's chalk or lead pencils. Felt and ball-point pens are too messy.

Scissors Keep one well-sharpened pair for fabric and a smaller pair for thread ends.

Rotary cutter Although not essential, this useful circular cutting device can cut several layers of fabric at once. For safety, use it only with a metal ruler which has a finger guard, and on an appropriate surface such as a cutting mat (p132).

Pins Fine brass lace pins will not mark the fabric.

Needles Have a selection of hand sewing needles: Sharps 8 or 9 are fine and long enough to take a number of stitches at a time.

Beeswax This is not essential, but pulling sewing thread along the wax strengthens the thread and helps it to slip through the fabric.

Thimble For hand sewing, it is best to use a thimble. Choose one which comfortably fits the second finger of your sewing hand.

Hoop While not absolutely essential, a hoop helps to keep appliqué work at an even tension. Choose a large embroidery hoop or a quilting hoop (see pp166–7).

Sewing machine This should make a good, even running stitch and should ideally have a back stitch, to prevent seams unravelling.

Seam ripper Used to unpick machined hems.

Iron A steam iron will press seams flatter than an ordinary one. Use a pressing cloth to avoid glazing the fabric.

FABRICS

Patchwork The most obvious choice of fabric for quiltmaking is a good quality, closely woven, dressweight pure cotton. It is pleasant to handle and sew, whether by hand or machine, and presses well. It washes easily, looks good and wears well, as many antique quilts testify, and has the additional advantage of being available in an almost limitless range of colours and patterns.

Pure cotton is not always easy to find in shops and stores. To obtain the exact colour it is often easier to make your selection from the wide ranges offered by specialist mail order companies. Cotton/polyester mixtures are more widely available but are generally less satisfactory because they are springy and give less crisp seams. When using a mixture of pure cotton and cotton/polyester fabrics, always set the iron to a low temperature for pressing.

There are other options besides cotton, however, and the choice will depend on the overall design, the sewing and quilting techniques, and the end use of the quilt or project. Silk and brocade have a richness and lustre which cotton lacks. Like cotton, they can be sewn by hand or machine, but are more difficult to handle and do not wear as well. Heavier fabrics such as corduroy, velvet, tweeds and suitings have more texture but are best reserved for machine stitching and designs with large, simple shapes. Always select fabrics of a similar weight for any one quilt, and check that their methods of cleaning are all compatible so that you do not end up having to dry clean a quilt just for the sake of a tiny proportion of the patches.

The most difficult fabrics to use are stretchy knits or shiny man-made fibres. Iron-on vilene can be used to stabilize a fabric of this sort but tends to give it a stiffer appearance.

Always pre-wash (washable) fabrics before marking and cutting to remove any dressing and to test for dye fastness and shrinkage.

Appliqué The range of fabrics which can be used for appliqué includes virtually anything which can be stitched and is certainly much broader than the patchwork range. In practice, however, there are certain limitations: fabrics that fray easily create obvious problems; fragile fabrics and ones which require dry cleaning restrict the wear of the quilt, and slippery or stretchy fabrics are difficult to sew. Many man-made fibres can be used, together with decorative strips of ribbon or lace, but for traditional, hand-sewn appliqué, dressweight pure cotton gives the best results.

Scrap bags Utility quilts in the past were often made from sewing scraps and the remnants of dresses, but these days it is often safer and easier to buy new fabrics when making a quilt, particularly if you are working with a definite design in mind. In this way, it is possible to make sure that your fabrics are compatible in type and weight. Some techniques, such as appliqué or crazy quilt-as-you-go (see p173), are more suitable for rag-bag projects than others, but even here it would be unwise to use a fabric without first testing it for washability and dye fastness. If you are using an old garment, simply cut away the seams, as the stitching makes these useless, and also reject any parts which are in the slightest degree worn, faded or stretched.

Buying and storing fabrics Attractive and fashionable prints and colours tend to go out of stock very rapidly and it is a good idea to buy a length of fabric when you see something which you like and store it for future use. On the other hand, you can save a lot of money by estimating how much of each fabric you will need for a quilt before buying. To do this, you need an accurate design drawing and the templates (see p135).

Fabrics are best kept as they are in stores: on a roll to stop creases forming. Cardboard tubes are available from stationery or art shops, as well as from the fabric shops themselves.

Marking and cutting Unless you are using part of a very intricate pattern, always mark on the wrong side of the fabric. Press the fabric and lay it on a flannelette sheet or a length of similar fabric to stop it slipping. Start by drawing a guideline about 12mm ($\frac{1}{2}$in) in from the selvedge (see p134) and lay the template against this line. Try to get as many sides of the template as possible running with the straight or cross grain (parallel to the selvedge or at right angles to it). Avoid the bias, which runs diagonally across the fabric and has the most stretch.

THREADS

Select a neutral colour which will blend in with the overall colour scheme. For hand sewing, use quilting thread, which makes strong stitches, or standard No. 50 cotton. For machining, use No. 40 cotton or, failing that, cotton/polyester; take care to match needle size to thread and to fabric. When you need a knotted thread in hand sewing, always knot the cut end so that during sewing the thread is pulled in the same direction in which it came off the reel: this will help to prevent knotting and twisting. Use tacking cotton for the tacking.

PATCHWORK TEMPLATES

Templates are the master shapes which are used to mark the outlines of the patches on the fabric ready for cutting out. They must be absolutely accurate, and although you can buy them, it is generally cheaper and more flexible to make your own, at least as far as the simpler shapes are concerned. If you decide to buy templates, make sure that they are the correct type for your chosen sewing method (see p134).

TEMPLATE MAKING EQUIPMENT

Graph paper It is far easier to draw accurate templates on isometric or squared graph paper.

Lead pencil A 2H pencil will give a fine line.

Metal ruler More accurate than wooden or plastic types, it is also safer to cut against.

Scalpel or craft knife Either of these can be used to cut card templates.

Card Use mounting card for hard-wearing templates for repeated patterns and thinner card for shapes which occur less frequently.

Spray glue This is formulated to allow for repositioning and does not buckle the paper.

Cutting mat This can be bought from art supply shops and is almost indestructible.

Dressmaker's ruler This is made from clear plastic and marked with a square grid and is invaluable for adding seam allowances.

Paper cutting scissors Paper blunts scissors, so never use your fabric scissors to cut paper.

WORKING DRAWING

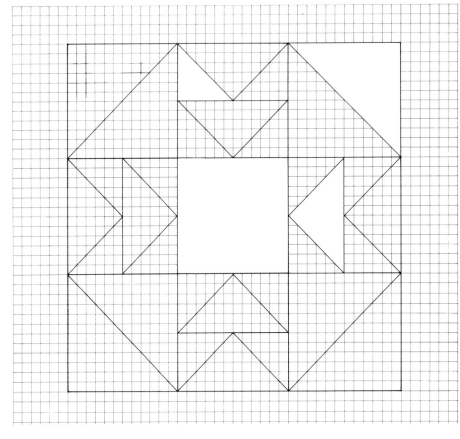

When you have decided on the design and size of the project, draw out a block or a section of the design which contains all the shapes to be used to the finished size, on graph paper. Use this drawing to check that all the pieces fit together precisely and for taking measurements when making the templates. You will need a template for each different shape in the pattern.

DRAWING A TEMPLATE

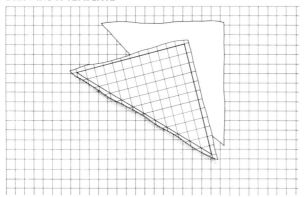

STICKING SHAPE TO CARD

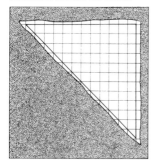

FINISHING THE TEMPLATE

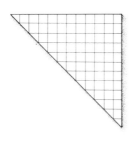

The templates used for this design were all cut from isometric graph paper. The more complex shapes in single colours are divided into smaller units for easier piecing, and the hexagon is made from a mirror image identical shape. Detail of 'Marriage Quilt' by Susan Carr.

DRAWING A TEMPLATE

The next stage is to draw each patch out, again to the finished size (in other words without seam allowances), on graph paper. If the template is to include seam allowances (see overleaf), add them, using the divisions of the graph paper or a dressmaker's ruler.

Cut the shape out with paper scissors, leaving at least 1cm (⅓in) round the marked edge. If you cut along the finished line at this stage, you will have to make this cut again when the guide has been stuck on the card (see next step), thereby doubling the risk of producing an inaccurate template.

STICKING SHAPE TO CARD

Using spray glue, spray the paper (not the card). A sheet of waste paper underneath will protect your surface. Use the spray lightly. Stick the paper shape to the card, making sure that it lies absolutely flat.

FINISHING THE TEMPLATE

Using a scalpel or craft knife and a metal ruler, carefully cut round the outer, marked edge of the template shape. Position the ruler outside the marked line so that if it accidentally slips you will be cutting into the card, not the template itself. Keep the knife almost parallel to the surface being cut and rest it against the ruler. Cut the card little by little until you are cleanly through.

When you have cut out all your templates, check them to make sure that they are accurately drawn and cut and will fit together. If they do not have seam allowances, check them against the full-scale graph drawing. If the templates include seam allowances, you will have to make up a sample piece of patchwork. If a template is going to be used many times, for example in an all-over one-patch design, it is a good idea to make several, so that these can be replaced if they get worn or bent.

WINDOW TEMPLATES

WINDOW TEMPLATES

These can be used, with either machine or hand sewing techniques, if the fabric has to be cut in a certain way, for example with a motif in the centre of a patch. Draw up the template, marking both the seam line (finished edge) and the cutting line (outer edge).

Place a paper outline on the card and cut out the inside shape to represent the finished patch. Then cut around the outer edge. This produces a frame which you can position over the fabric (lay the fabric right side up) before drawing round the outer edge and then cutting out the patch.

SEAM ALLOWANCES

Whether your templates should or should not include a seam allowance will depend largely on your chosen sewing method. Keep to the same seam allowance throughout: most people prefer 6mm ($\frac{1}{4}$in), but some choose 9mm ($\frac{3}{8}$in).

CHOOSING THE RIGHT TEMPLATE

1 For hand sewing with a running stitch (pp138–9), cut templates to the finished patch size. The outer edge of the template will then mark the seam line. The cutting edge must then be drawn in when the fabric is marked to give the seam allowance. Leave 6mm ($\frac{1}{4}$ in) around each shape for this (see p 138).

2 For hand sewing using backing papers, cut two templates. One is the size of the finished patch plus a seam allowance all round. This is used for cutting the fabric. The

second is the finished size of the patch, without the seam allowance, and is used to cut backing papers.

3 Templates for machine sewn patchwork (pp142–3) generally include seam allowances because the presser foot can be used as a guide for the sewing line, which therefore does not need to be marked in. If, however, you are making an intricate piece of machine patchwork with many small pieces, it may be easier to use templates to the finished size and then mark the cutting line on the fabric, as for hand sewing.

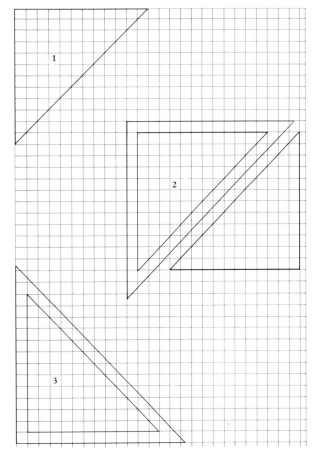

DIAMOND TEMPLATES

Stars made up from diamond shapes linked together are a popular patchwork theme. Two main shapes are used: the wide diamond, which makes a six-pointed star and which can easily be drawn on isometric graph paper, and the narrower diamond, which is used to make an eight-pointed star. For the latter, either buy a ready-made template or draw one, as shown here.

NARROW DIAMOND
Draw a line, AB, which should be drawn to the desired length for one side of the star shape. Using a protractor or set square, draw another line, AC, at a 45° angle to AB and the same length as AB. Setting your compasses to this length, make two intersecting arcs, from points B and C, to find point D. Join BD and DC to complete the long diamond.

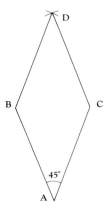

ASYMMETRICAL TEMPLATES

When using asymmetrical shapes, take care to mark your material correctly, reversing the template as necessary, especially when using fabric with obvious right and wrong sides.

ONE-WAY SHAPES
To mark and cut shapes using a non-reversible template, place the template wrong side up on the fabric's wrong side.

MIRROR IMAGES
In many cases, a one-way or irregularly-shaped template is used to cut mirror image patches, making a pair. Keep the fabric wrong side up and use the template first wrong side then right side up.

ONE-WAY SHAPES

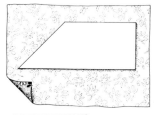

MIRROR IMAGES

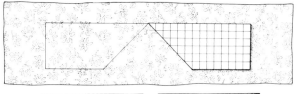

COMPLETING EDGES

Sometimes a one-patch all-over pattern, such as a traditional hexagon design, may need to have some extra shapes added round the edges if the patchwork is to be squared off for use as a quilt top. It is, of course, possible to leave an irregular diamond- or hexagon-shaped edge, but this would mean that the wadding and backing would also have to be cut to shape, and the irregular edges separately bound. Alternatively, the patchwork might be appliquéd to a straight-edged background fabric and then joined to the other layers.

EDGING TEMPLATES
Make a full-size drawing of a corner and edge section of your design on graph paper. This will show the additional shapes needed. Although they may appear to be just a section of your main template – for example, a half hexagon or the half shapes along a diagonally set block – you cannot simply cut fabric patches in half as there would be no seam allowance along the cut edge. It is therefore necessary to make new templates for each additional shape. Use your scale diagram to draw each shape in the usual way, adding seam allowances.

To complete the side edges of 'Tailor's Stars', Iona Heath cut half-triangular templates and reversed them to make the necessary mirror images on alternate rows.

ESTIMATING FABRIC

Referring to your design drawing, note the number of times any one template will be used for each fabric. Note also any plain blocks, lattice strips and borders. To work out the quantity for any given shape, you will need first to know whether your proposed fabric is 90cm (36in) or 115cm (45in) wide. Take away the selvedges, and do not forget to add seam allowances around the templates, if not already included. To calculate, divide the number of times the template depth fits across the fabric width into the total number of patches needed in that fabric; multiply the result by the template width. Calculate odd template shapes, such as appliqué leaves, to the nearest geometrical shape.

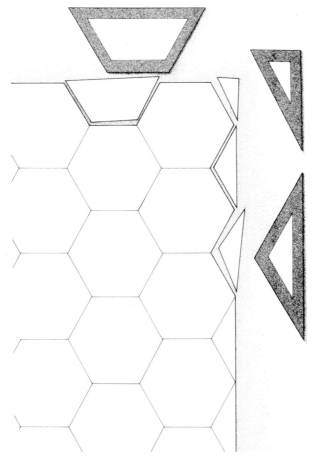

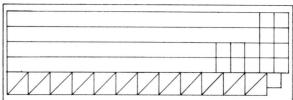

SCALED-DOWN CUTTING LAYOUT
A more accurate way of estimating fabrics is to use a scaled-down cutting layout. Position the largest or longest shapes, such as borders or lattice strips first, and butt smaller pieces in between. Keep all the shapes parallel with the edge of the cutting layout.

135

PATCHWORK SEWING SEQUENCE

The sewing method and sequence should be considered at the design stage, but must be worked out in detail before you begin sewing. Apart from backing paper patterns, which have to be sewn by hand, most designs have straight seams and the patches can be sewn together by hand or machine. If the pattern entails sewing into a corner, it is easier to do this by hand: always sew away from the corner in each direction, but avoid designs with sharp angles.

Whatever the design, the aim is to keep to a sewing sequence which will break the work up into manageable blocks or units, so that only at the very end are you piecing together large sections to make the full-size top.

BLOCKS

Most blocks fall into a square grid, but some grids are easier to identify than others. For example, in the Jack-in-the-Box block featured here, which is based on a five-patch (25-square) grid, each corner appears to contain four small triangles and a single, odd-shaped patch. In fact, however, the latter is made from two separate patches, making the sewing more straightforward.

The central cross is made from four different strips joined to a central square. Although it would be possible to join two shorter strips to one long one, the square gives a much neater and more balanced appearance.

WORKING OUT THE SEQUENCE

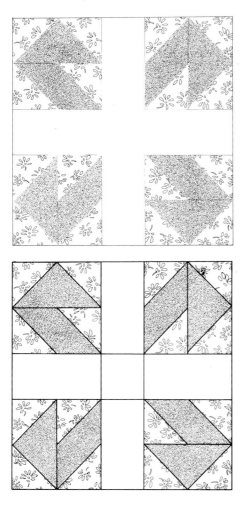

WORKING OUT
THE SEQUENCE
Before joining the patches, lay them out in the pattern of the finished block. (Note that the shapes illustrated here are the size of the finished patches and do not include seam allowances.) Although most of the patches are initially joined into rectangles, it is easy to see that the design is based on a grid of five squares across and five down.

JOINING THE PATCHES
1 *Sew the smaller units together to make the eight pieced rectangles for the corner sections.*

2 *Join pairs of rectangles to make the corner squares.*

3 *Sew the units together into three rows.*

4 *Sew the rows together to complete the block.*

JOINING THE PATCHES

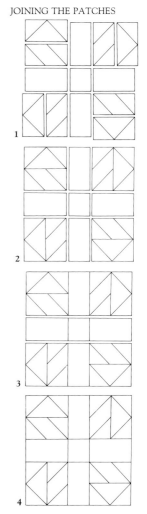

ALIGNING PATCHES

In most cases, patches are sewn together with the cut edges in alignment; for example, when two triangles of equal size are joined into a square or when squares or strips are joined. With joins that run at angles, however, remember that it is always the seam lines, not the cut edges, which must be aligned. If the seam line is marked, the positioning is easy to work out, but it is more difficult with machine sewing, when the patches are unmarked and you have to allow an overlap.

JOINING TRIANGLES INTO RECTANGLES
For each seam in turn, lay the patches right sides together, so that the seam lines are directly over one another. The top edges align, but the smaller triangles overlap at the bottom. When the unit is pressed, the point of the larger triangle lies on the seam line.

JOINING TRIANGLES OR DIAMONDS INTO ROWS
Match the seam lines, not cut edges, as shown, so that the point of the uppermost shape projects at the top.

INCORRECT ALIGNMENT

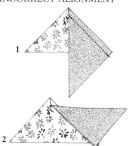

INCORRECT ALIGNMENT
With seams that join angled patches to one another, it is a mistake to match the cut edges rather than the seam lines. If so, when you open the patches out flat after sewing them together, you will find that instead of a straight edge, you will have produced an unwanted stepped effect, with one patch lower than the other.

JOINING TRIANGLES INTO ROWS

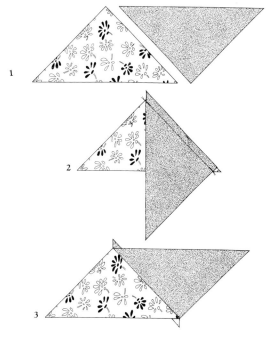

JOINING TRIANGLES INTO RECTANGLES

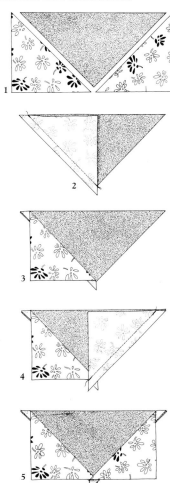

JOINING DIAMONDS INTO ROWS

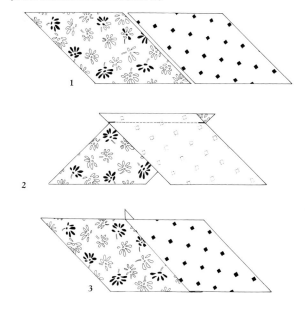

SEWING PATCHWORK BY HAND

MARKING THE FABRIC

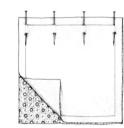

CUTTING OUT

RUNNING STITCH METHOD

This is the method used for hand sewing repeated block patterns and is also the easiest way of sewing curved seams. It is much quicker than the backing paper method of hand sewing (see p140) and it produces a similarly gentle, soft-edged effect, well suited to traditional-type patterns. The seam line is marked in and the allowance is usually 6mm ($\frac{1}{4}$in), especially if the finished patches are 5cm (2in) across or less, but you can take an allowance of 9mm ($\frac{3}{8}$in) for a stronger, bulkier seam. The basic method can be adapted to machine sewing, but with the stitching extending into the seam allowance.

SEWING PATCHES TOGETHER

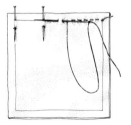

MARKING THE FABRIC
Using a rule and a well sharpened coloured pencil, draw a line on the wrong side of the fabric, parallel to the selvedge. (Leave space to add seam allowances.) Position the template at one corner, with one edge lying on the line, and draw round it, making sure that the corners are well defined. Add a seam allowance all round, position the template one seam allowance away from the outer edge, and repeat. Work across the fabric, making sure that

the patches butt up against each other as much as possible, even when you change to a different template.

CUTTING OUT
Use well sharpened fabric scissors and carefully cut round the outer marked edge of each patch (the inner marked edge will be the seam line). The more you have been able to align the patches, the quicker it will be to cut them out. Always cut the fabric; never tear it, as this will fray the edges and pull the patches

out of shape. As you cut, sort the patches into piles, according to shape and colour.

SEWING PATCHES TOGETHER
Place two corresponding patches right sides together, so that the marked sewing line is on the outside. Pin the patches together, placing a pin at each corner first, and then at intervals along the line. All pins should be inserted at right angles to the marked sewing line. Sew with a length of thread about 35cm (14in) long, with a knot at the cut

end. Remove the corner pin and insert the needle at the same point: on no account sew through the seam allowances. Sew with a small, even running stitch, checking from time to time that you are following the marked line on both patches and removing the pins as you go. Stitch to the end of the marked line and then finish off with two or three back stitches.

SEWING ROWS TOGETHER

When you have joined the patches into rows, the rows can then be stitched together, using the same method as for individual patches. Place two rows with right sides together, then put a pin at each end of the row and at the points where seams meet. Add extra pins where needed along the marked sewing line, and sew the rows together with a small, even running stitch, removing the pins as you go. Avoid sewing through seam allowances, as before, and continually check that the stitching line is falling on the marked seam line on both sides of the work. Join the rows in batches so that you do not have to handle a large area until the final stages.

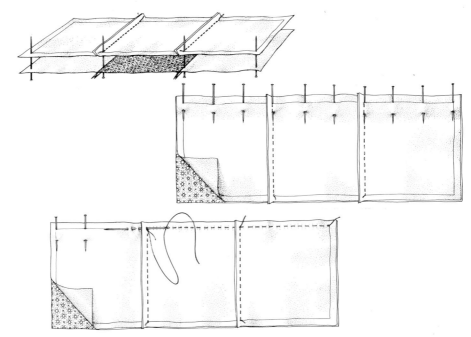

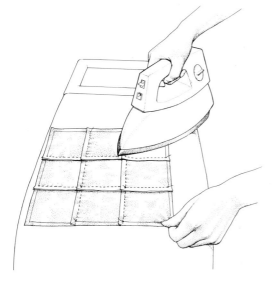

PRESSING

Hand sewn seams are always stronger if they are pressed to one side rather than open. The usual practice is to press them to the darker side so that the seam allowances will not show through. An alternative method is to press all the seams in one direction only. Whichever way you choose to press the seams, this job should be left to the end, so that you do not have to sew through several seam allowances together at points where patches meet. Pressing a

completed top can be difficult, so press each block or unit as it is completed, then press rows as they are joined: this will lessen the total amount of pressing at the finish. Always press the back of the work first, then lightly iron the right side, using a well-padded ironing board and a cloth to avoid marking and stretching the fabric.

Most traditional American quilts were hand sewn with a small running stitch. The quilts were functional and utilitarian and it was too labour-intensive to back each patch with a separate paper template. The running stitch used less cotton, and suited both the straight lines of the geometric patterns and the large patches and strips.

This is a typical everyday scrap-bag quilt, using extra fabric for the lattice strips and border. The Roman Cross block is a four-patch design that can be subdivided into 64 squares. Each block here is made from scraps of a different fabric, but the design is unified by virtue of the lattice strips and border in a strong single colour.

Even after the sewing machine came into general use around 1865, quilts were still very often sewn by hand.

BACKING PAPER METHOD

This is the most precise patchwork technique and is used to build up decorative inlaid mosaic designs. It is suitable for more intricate shapes, such as hexagons or diamonds with fine points, but it takes considerably longer than the other methods, each patch being tacked over a backing paper and sewn to its neighbour with overcast stitches. Appliqué can also be made in this way, in which case the backing papers are removed when the backing fabric is cut away from behind the shapes (p149). Although this type of patchwork is associated with mosaic patterns, it can be used for repeated blocks; but you must stick to either this or the running stitch method.

BACKING PAPERS

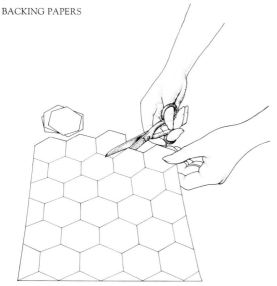

FABRIC PATCHES

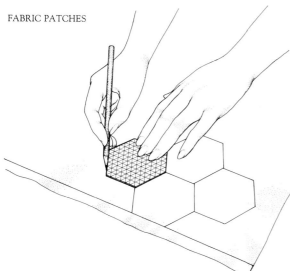

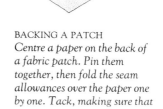

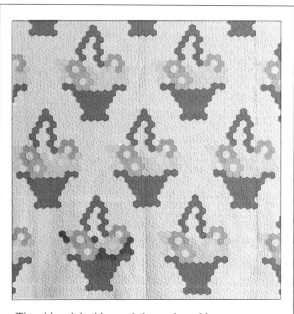

BACKING A PATCH
Centre a paper on the back of a fabric patch. Pin them together, then fold the seam allowances over the paper one by one. Tack, making sure that the corners are sharp. (Leave both ends of the thread free, so that the stitches can easily be pulled out later.) Remove the pin and press the patch to define the sewing edge.

BACKING PAPERS
Using the smaller template, mark writing paper to make backing papers. Butt the shapes against each other to ensure that they fit. You can use photocopies of your original sheet, but do not mix these with hand-drawn papers.

FABRIC PATCHES
Place the larger template on the reverse side of the fabric and carefully draw along each edge. Butt the shapes together and try to keep the grain of the fabric running in the same direction for each patch. Cut the patches out one by one.

This old quilt builds motifs from coloured hexagons on a pale pink ground, and uses them as a repeated image. The usual flowers made from rosettes of hexagons are confined in the skilfully composed baskets, the pastel shades relieved by the occasional splash of green foliage. Each hexagon is quilted, giving texture to an otherwise plain surface.

SEWING PATCHES TOGETHER
Place two patches right sides together, making sure that the edges match. Thread your needle with about 32cm (13in) of quilting thread and knot the end you have just cut (this helps to prevent tangling). Insert the needle through one corner of the upper patch, losing the knot under the seam allowance, then sew the patches together with small regular overcast stitches. When the patches are opened out, the stitches will be just visible from the front. Finish with several reversed stitches.

MAKING STAR PATTERNS

Many designs associated with the backing paper method incorporate six- or eight-pointed stars, made by joining diamond-shaped patches. It is important that the patches should be arranged as shown below so that they lie flat at the centre point and there is no hole where they meet.

SEWING PATCHES TOGETHER

ASSEMBLING DIAMONDS

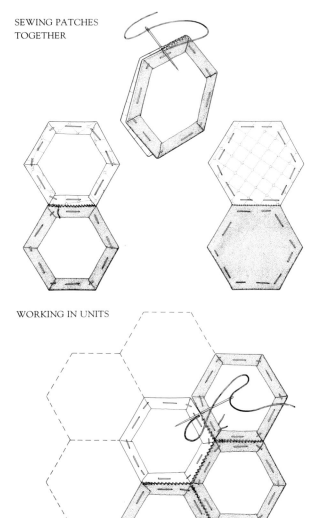

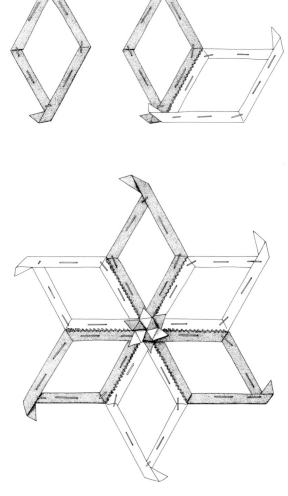

WORKING IN UNITS

WORKING IN UNITS
Join patches into units, such as rosettes, which can then be sewn together to make a larger piece. To make a rosette, work from the centre outwards. Start by joining the centre patch to the one which will lie immediately below it, then add a third patch to the first two and continue in an anti-clockwise direction until all seven patches have been sewn together. Press them flat. Remove the backing papers only when all the sides on each patch have been joined to other patches or the edging.

ASSEMBLING DIAMONDS
Prepare the patches in the usual way but allow the seams to lie flat at the acute angles. When sewing the patches together, make sure that the tails follow in the same direction as each other and do not stitch beyond the point defined by the backing paper. Join patches to make the two halves of the star, then join the half stars into one, working from the centre outwards in each direction. Press the work on the reverse side, allowing the tails to interlock. Lightly press the top.

MACHINE SEWING PATCHWORK

It is much quicker to join pieces by machine than by hand, not only because of the obvious speed of the stitching itself, but also because you can dispense with the business of marking the sewing lines on every patch. The distance between the needle and the outer edge of the presser foot produces a consistent seam allowance: on most machines this is conveniently 6mm (¼ in), and provided the pieces are cut accurately and with clean straight edges, you simply align the raw edge of the fabric with the edge of the presser foot to get your seam allowance. It is worth adjusting the templates for a slightly larger seam if the distance is, say, 9mm (⅜ in), but anything under 6mm makes too narrow a seam. In this case, align the raw edge with a length of masking tape stuck on the base plate 6mm away from the needle.

Seams must be pressed open as the work progresses, so have an iron set up near the sewing machine to maintain your speed of work.

MARKING AND CUTTING

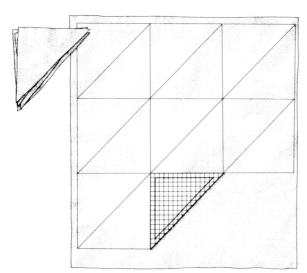

SEWING

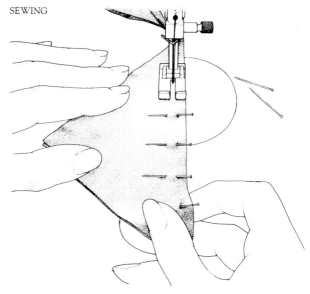

CUTTING
SEVERAL LAYERS
OF FABRIC

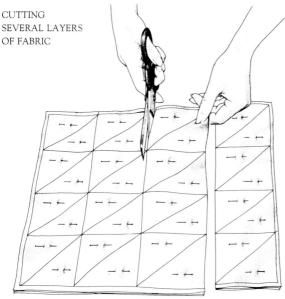

MARKING AND CUTTING
Since there is no sewing line to follow, the fabric must be marked accurately and cut with clean straight edges to make sure that the patches fit together well. Press the fabric flat and lay it right side down.

Place the template in the top left-hand corner and carefully draw around it. Butt the next and subsequent outlines up against one another, leaving no gaps. When all the patches in that fabric have been marked, cut them out.

CUTTING SEVERAL
LAYERS OF FABRIC
Although it is obviously most accurate to mark and cut each fabric individually, it is possible to cut identical patches in several layers of fabric at once if your scissors are sharp. Take up to six fabrics, all the same size, and select the one which is easiest to mark. Mark the template outlines on the wrong side of this fabric and place it on top of the other fabrics, all with their wrong sides up. Pin them together, placing a pin in each patch to stop the layers shifting. Cut through all the layers at once and remove pins.

SEWING
Set your machine to 5 stitches per centimetre (10–12 per inch). Place two patches right sides together and put a pin at either end of the (unmarked)

SEWING IDENTICAL UNITS

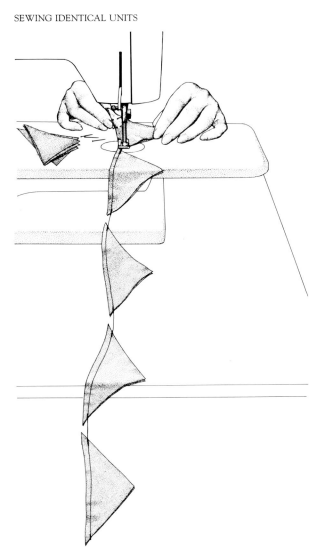

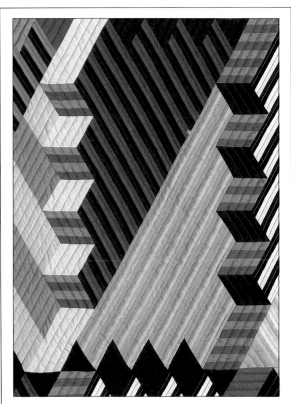

Detail from 'Stripy Step' (pp 60–1). Design is Pauline Burbidge's quiltmaking priority. She uses unswervingly accurate machine stitching to maintain the geometrical precision of her shapes. She likes Hunan silk for its steely luminosity which is appropriate to her mechanistic images, emphasized here by the different blues and black, and for handling well, making crisp unbulky seams. The speed of the sewing machine gives this quiltmaker some chance of keeping pace with her teeming design ideas.

seamline, and several in between. Pins inserted at right angles to the seamline are easier to remove as sewing progresses: take them out before they go under the presser foot. When sewing, position patches so that the cut edge aligns with the edge of the presser foot or masking tape and the needle drops on the seamline, making the 6mm (¼ in) seam allowance automatically. Make a few back stitches at either end of the seam.

SEWING IDENTICAL UNITS
A number of identical patches can be sewn with a continuous thread and separated later to save time. Pin the pairs of

patches together in the usual way and begin and end each seam with back stitching, but instead of cutting the thread simply raise the presser foot and needle and pull the threads slightly before feeding the next pair through. When you have stitched a long chain of patches, separate them, trim the threads and press the seams open.

SEWING UNITS TOGETHER
Always press seams open before moving on to the next stage and joining larger units or rows of patches together. Position pins at either end of the sewing line, in the centre, and matching any seams, then add extra pins in between.

SEWING UNITS TOGETHER

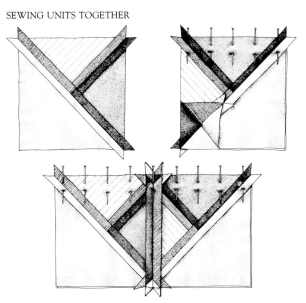

QUICK PATCHWORK METHOD

Some quiltmakers appear to feel that the success of a patchwork depends on the time put into making it, but in fact there are several quick methods which can speed up the process without in any way altering the visual impact, and I firmly believe in using these short cuts whenever possible. In the quick technique shown here, which can be used for patterns based on large or small triangles, rectangles and squares, two large pieces of fabric are pinned and stitched together, so that only the top one need be marked with patches and a great deal less time is also spent in cutting.

This method is suitable for hand sewing, using a running stitch, but is ideal for machine work. Use the presser foot of your machine as a guide when sewing (see p142), but if this gives a width of less than 6mm (¼in) or you are hand sewing, then use a dressmaker's ruler to mark the sewing lines on the fabric. Make a single block to start with and check it against the design.

MAKING UP
THE **A** PATCHES

FINISHING THE **A** PATCHES

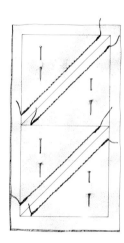

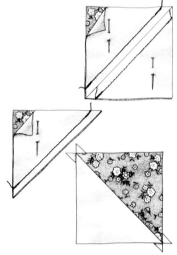

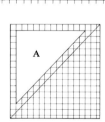

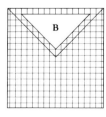

MAKING THE TEMPLATES
*Accuracy is essential to this technique, so start by drawing the block to the finished size on graph paper so that it can be referred to for template measurements. Decide how many templates are needed and draw each to the finished size on graph paper. Add a 6mm (¼in) seam allowance round each. For patch **A** (a half square), double the triangle so that the template becomes a square. For patch **B** (a quarter square), make a square of four equal triangles. Patch **C** is left as it is. Stick the graph paper onto a piece of cardboard and cut out the three templates in the usual way (see p133).*

MAKING UP THE **A** PATCHES
*Cut two different fabrics to the same size, making sure that they can accommodate template **A** twice, as shown. Place the fabrics right sides together, with the one which is easiest to mark on top. Draw round the template twice, butting the edges together. Add the diagonal line to each square. Pin the fabrics together, placing a pin in each triangle, away from the pencilled lines. Set the machine to 5 stitches per centimetre (10–12 per inch) and stitch 6mm (¼in) in from either side of the diagonal. Begin and end with several back stitches. Repeat for the second square.*

FINISHING THE **A** PATCHES
Cut round the edges of the two squares, following the marked lines. Cut across each square along the diagonal, remove the pins and press each pair of patches flat, with the seam open (or to one side if the work is being sewn by hand).

144

B PATCHES

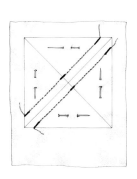

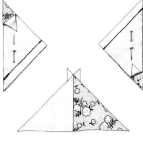

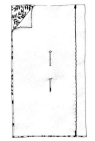

C PATCHES

MAKING
MULTIPLE UNITS

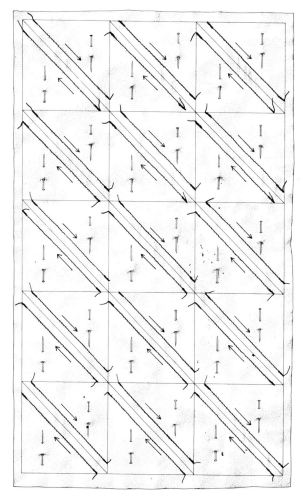

MAKING UP THE B PATCHES
Prepare the two chosen fabrics and place them right sides together. Draw round template B once only, on the top fabric. Add two diagonals and pin the fabrics together, with a pin in each of the four triangles. Stitch 6mm (¼in) in from each side of one diagonal only. Begin and end with several back stitches. Also back stitch when crossing the diagonal.

Cut round the outside edge, then along both diagonal lines, making four pairs of patches. Remove the pins and open out two opposite pairs. Press the seams flat and sew the patches together in the usual way. The two extra pairs can be used at a later stage.

MAKING UP THE C PATCHES
Prepare two fabrics, then take the top fabric wrong side up and draw round the template twice, butting the short edges together to make one long strip. Pin the fabrics together, putting a pin in each rectangle. Stitch 6mm (¼in) in from the marked line down one long edge. Back stitch at the beginning and end and at each of the intersecting horizontal lines to stop the stitches unravelling when cut.

First cut round the outer edge and then along the horizontal lines. Remove the pins and open out the pairs of patches, then press the seams open. This method can easily be adapted to make squares.

MAKING MULTIPLE UNITS
When you have made sufficient patches and sewn one block together to check that your templates are correct, you can then start to sew large numbers of patches together in groups, enough for several blocks. Using the above method, up to a metre of fabric can be sewn at one time. (A metre is about as much fabric as can be handled at one go: more would tend to slip during machining, pulling the patches out of shape.)

Make sure that units butt up against each other, to speed up marking and cutting, but always back stitch at the beginning and end of each patch. To avoid constantly turning the fabric: stitch in one direction (left of the marked diagonals), then turn and work down the other side. To avoid stitching across the tops of adjacent triangles, stop at the end of each marked patch, lift the presser foot, raise the needle, gently pull the threads over to the next patch and restart. The resulting loops can be cut and trimmed later. Cut and press the finished patches as already shown.

LOG
CABIN

This is one of the simplest patchwork patterns to make, but at the same time it has enormous design potential because the blocks can be arranged in any number of ways to create different over-all patterns. Traditionally, the block is divided diagonally into a light and a dark half, or a contrast of colours, and it has a plain coloured patch at the centre.

Log Cabin can be made by hand or machine, and is an excellent scrap-bag project, since only a comparatively small amount of fabric is needed for the centre squares and strips. The finished strips are usually about 2.5cm (1in), but it is possible to buy Perspex strips of varying widths to use as templates, or you can draw the strips on the fabric with a ruler and a coloured pencil.

STITCHING SEQUENCE

1

2

3

4

PREPARING THE PIECES

finished block

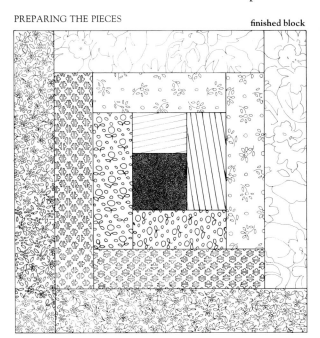

PREPARING THE PIECES
Only one template is needed: the one used for the centre square, which is generally about twice as wide as the strips (finished size) plus seam allowances. The number of strips around the square will vary according to the size of the project and the availability of suitable fabrics, but make sure that you have an equal number either of light and dark fabrics or of fabrics in two contrast colours. When you have marked and cut patches for the centre squares, cut strips from the remaining fabrics. The strips should be of equal width (the size of the finished strip plus two seam allowances) and are easiest to work with if they are some 38 to 46cm (15 to 18in) in length.

STITCHING SEQUENCE
Take one square and trim a strip of another fabric to the same length as the square. With right sides facing, pin and stitch the two together 1. Press the seam so that the strip lies flat. Taking the same fabric as the first strips, cut a second strip to the length of the square plus the first strip 2. Pin, stitch and press open, as before. Now take a strip from the contrasting group of fabrics and cut it to the length of the square plus the previous strip, then pin and stitch it in position, working clockwise round the square 3. Use the same fabric or category to complete the first round 4. Continue in this way until the required size is reached.

DIAMOND LOG CABIN

The Log Cabin technique of sewing strips around a central square can be adapted to other shapes, such as triangles, hexagons and diamonds. The narrow diamond used to make an eight-pointed star is the shape illustrated here. Remember that with a pattern built up from such non-square blocks you will need to make large right-angled triangle and square templates to fill in the edges so that you end up with regular square blocks with which to make up your quilt.

STITCHING SEQUENCE

wrong side   **right side**

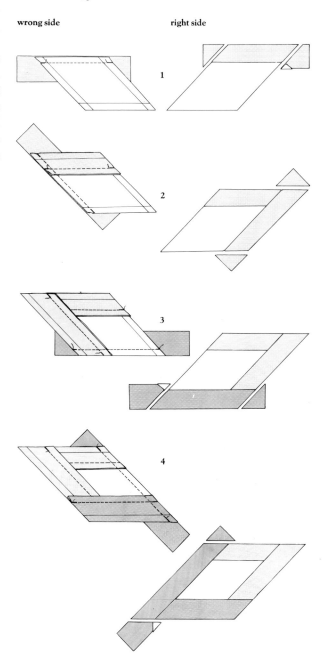

PREPARING THE PIECES   **finished block**

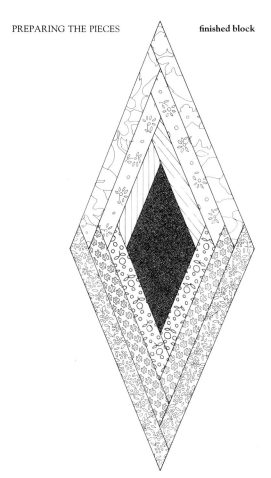

PREPARING THE PIECES
When working with shapes such as diamonds which are not made up of right angles, it is easier to make sure that the strips lie correctly if you trim them after stitching and pressing, rather than precutting them as for a square Log Cabin block. Make a template for the central patches and mark and cut out

the fabric. From the fabrics chosen for strips, cut lengths as wide as the finished strip plus two seam allowances.

STITCHING SEQUENCE
With right sides of fabric together, pin the first strip along one side of the central diamond patch, leaving an ample allowance for an overlap at the ends. Work with

the diamond wrong side uppermost, so that you can see where to begin and end the stitching: it should go across the top edge of the diamond, including seam allowances. Sew the first strip to the diamond, securing both ends with back stitching 1.

Press open, keeping the strip flat and folding the diamond back, as shown, so that the

work now lies flat. Trim the strip at an angle so that it forms a continuation of the diamond shape. Sew the second strip across the second side of the diamond patch and across the width of the first strip 2. Press and then trim, as before. Join subsequent strips in the same way, pressing each one flat before trimming it to the exact shape (3 and 4).

APPLIQUE

It is very much a matter of individual taste whether you prefer to make appliqué or patchwork. In general, appliqué is associated with a more free-flowing and less geometrical approach to quiltmaking. The possibility of using curved shapes means it is more suitable than patchwork for pictorial designs, though many modern designers (myself among them) have been attracted to patchwork partly because of its abstract qualities. Appliqué, on the other hand, offers an almost painterly scope of deploying fabrics on a background to depict representational designs.

An appliqué image can either be used on a large scale to fill the entire quilt area or used on smaller units to make a repeated block pattern, which means that you can also use the quilt-as-you-go technique (p172).

Another advantage of appliqué is that although pure dressweight cotton is always a favourite for appliqué quiltmaking, a much wider range of fabrics can be used and can all be incorporated into the same design. This is because the pieces are all stitched to a background fabric instead of to each other, as in patchwork, and it therefore does not matter so much if they have varying degrees of weight and stretch. The finished quilt may have to be dry cleaned, but it will have an extra tactile and visual dimension.

It is easier to make successful hand appliqué if you use a hoop (see pp166–7), which helps to keep the fabric at an even tension and prevents it from pulling out of true, but apart from this, the same equipment is needed as for patchwork.

APPLIQUE TEMPLATES

Unless the fabric is cut freehand, a template is needed for each individual applied shape (bias strips can be used for curved lines and stems). Whether the stitching is worked by hand or machine, the templates are always made to the size of the completed patch (without seam allowances). The easiest way is to make a full-scale drawing of the design, then to draw each of the shapes on tracing paper, numbering each shape on the design and on the tracing, so that the design drawing can act as a reference during work. You can use the tracing paper shapes as templates

but it is usually better to stick them on thin card. If the template is to be used several times, for example in a repeated block design, it may be preferable to choose a thicker card.

Where shapes overlap, for instance if a leaf is partly hidden behind a stem, as in the design shown overleaf, you should make the template for the entire shape and then tuck it under the overlapping shape.

MARKING AND CUTTING

STAY STITCHING

MARKING AND CUTTING
Place the template right side up on the right side of the fabric. Mark around the edge (this will be the fold/stitching line) in well sharpened pencil of a colour similar to that of the fabric. Add a 6mm ($\frac{1}{4}$in) seam allowance all round. When marking out a number of patches, leave some space in between so that they are easy to handle when stay stitching. Roughly cut out each patch, not too close to the outer marked line.

STAY STITCHING
Stay stitching is not absolutely essential but it makes it easier to turn the edges under neatly. Use a short stitch length and work with the right side of the fabric uppermost. Machine stitch in the seam allowance, just outside the inner line (you can stay stitch by hand, using a small running stitch, if this is more convenient).

CUTTING THE EDGES

TACKING

This 'Cherry Basket' pattern combines appliqué with patchwork. Usually the cherries (or more often flowers) are seen sprouting from the top of the basket, but this maker could not resist interpreting them in her own way and applying them to the pieced triangles of the basket itself. The curved handles are also applied.

STITCHING

FINISHING

CUTTING THE EDGES

Cut out each shape along the outer marked edge. If the edges are curved, finish them as shown so that they lie flat when turned under. For outer curves, cut out pieces so that there are no tucks of excess fabric when the seam allowance is turned under. For inner edges, clip the seam allowance up to the stay stitching. At an inside angle, clip into the corner. At any outer corners cut across to reduce the bulk.

TACKING

In order to produce accurate edges, it is essential to tack each piece. Work with the right side uppermost and fold the seam allowance under, following the inner marked line. Press the edge firmly with your fingers to crease it, then hold it in place with small tacking stitches. Make sure that the stay stitching is within the seam allowance and cannot be seen on the right side. Make curved edges appear as smooth as possible.

STITCHING

Press the backing fabric well. It may help to first fold the fabric diagonally into quarters and press lightly to mark the centre point. Pin each shape in position and tack it in place with vertical stitches. Sew it to the background with a small, neat, regularly spaced overcast stitch, using a thread which matches the appliqué fabric. Begin with a knot hidden in the seam allowance and finish with one between the top and backing fabric.

FINISHING

Remove tacking and press when sewing is complete. If the work is to be quilted, it is easier and looks much better if the backing fabric is removed behind the applied image, and it also avoids the possibility of a darker background fabric showing through a lighter shape. With small sharp scissors, carefully cut away the backing fabric up to within 6mm (¼in) of the stitching line on the reverse side of the work, behind each shape.

OVERLAPPING SHAPES

Some of the most attractive appliqué patterns have several elements which lap over or under one another. Work out a sensible order of sewing before tacking the shapes in position.

TEMPLATES

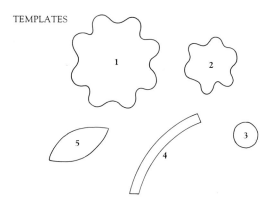

SEWING SEQUENCE

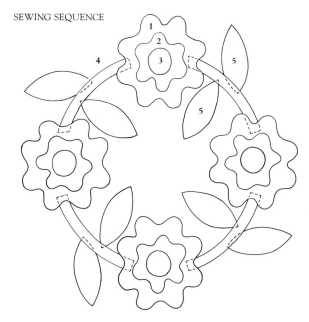

'Poppyfield' is typical of appliqué images built up with several overlapping shapes to give a richer, more elaborate effect. The main poppy flower would have been worked on first, starting with the background shapes and working through to those at the front.

REMOVING BACKING FABRIC   **wrong side**

TEMPLATES
Start by drawing the design to the full size and deciding how many templates are needed. Templates **1** and **2** include the central portion, although this will be covered. The links which bind the composition together could be cut with a template **4** or, depending on the size of the finished design, you might use bias strips. Templates **4** and **5** are both cut so that the ends of the fabric patches can be tucked under the overlying pieces.

SEWING SEQUENCE
Start by preparing the patches in the usual way. Fold the background fabric diagonally into quarters and lightly press to give guidelines for positioning the pieces. Position the main flower shapes **1**. Link these with the stem shapes **4**, tucking the ends under the flowers, then finish by positioning the leaves, tucking one end of each leaf under a stem. Tack the pieces in position, then start by sewing the large flowers **1**. Carefully cut away the background fabric behind the flower (see preceding page), then tack and sew the central petal shape **2** and cut away behind this, as shown in the diagram. Finish by sewing the centres **3** and cutting away a portion of fabric, patch **2**, from behind it. Stitch the stems next, and then the leaves **5**.

REMOVING THE BACKING FABRIC
Using small, sharp scissors, carefully cut away the backing fabric 6mm ($\frac{1}{4}$in) inside the stitched edge. Where possible, for example in the case of the leaves, work outwards (in this instance from the stems to the points) so that any excess fabric can be eased out and the overall work will lie flat.

Although it is not absolutely necessary to cut away fabric behind the shapes, when several layers are involved the quilting would not show up unless the lower layers were removed from behind the uppermost shapes.

MACHINE SEWING APPLIQUE

In machine appliqué, the shapes are attached with close zigzag (satin) stitch, giving them very clearly defined outlines and producing a totally different visual effect to that of hand appliqué. Although the machine technique is quicker than hand work it is by no means an easy option and it is a good idea to make some practice pieces before embarking on a project with many curved and angled seams. The patches are cut to the finished size, without seam allowances, and the raw edges are then hidden by the stitching. If you are lucky enough to have a machine with additional embroidery stitches, then this facility can be put to good use to embellish your work, but it is more important that the machine should make a good, even zigzag stitch. If not, you can follow the first four steps of the hand sewing method and then stitch close to the edge of the applied pieces with a small machine running stitch, creating a less strongly defined outline.

SEWING SEQUENCE

1 *Cut out the shape (do not include a seam allowance) and pin it in position on the background fabric.*

2 *Tack the shape in position, keeping fairly close to the edge.*

3 *With the machine set to a close zigzag stitch, machine round the edge of the shape. On edges which are not straight the foot must frequently be raised, with the needle down to hold the fabric, and the work eased round to allow a smooth sewing line. Always avoid back stitching: pull threads to the back of the work and finish off by hand. The zigzag stitch will probably hide the tacking stitches, but if not these must be removed. If* any of the raw edge or loose threads of fabric are still showing, trim them with small sharp scissors.

Add any further decoration, for example the outline of the body of the butterfly and the division between the wings, using whichever machine stitch seems appropriate. As far as possible, work from the centre of the shape towards the outer edges, to ease out any extra fabric and avoid puckers.

SEWING SEQUENCE

HAWAIIAN APPLIQUE

In Hawaiian appliqué, a single motif is applied to a background fabric. The original Hawaiian motifs were very large and intricate and were made to the size of a full-scale quilt. These designs took a high degree of expertise to complete, but the technique can easily be adapted to a scale of block that is much more manageable in size.

It is possible to buy templates, but it is more interesting to make your own individual designs by folding and marking paper squares, as shown below. The resulting snowflake shapes generally look best if, like traditional Hawaiian quilts, they are stitched by hand and are worked in plain coloured cotton fabrics with bright, eye-catching contrasts in strong primary colours. The shapes may be emphasized by contoured quilting.

MAKING THE TEMPLATE
Experiment by making several folded paper patterns. Make sure that your final design is not so narrow at any point that you will have difficulty in turning the edges under.

1 Take a square of paper as large as you want the finished appliqué design to be. Fold it in eighths as shown, so that you finish up with all the cut edges on one side and all the folded edges on the other side of the final diagonal.

2 Draw a design on the folded paper, similar to that
illustrated. Always make sure that your design connects on the diagonal and on the folded edge on the right.

3 Unfold the design and use one-eighth as a template.

MARKING AND CUTTING
Take a square of fabric the same size as the paper and fold it the same way into eighths. Keep the wrong side outside. Press lightly. Pin the paper template to the folded fabric, making sure that the edges meet exactly. Trace round the shape and cut it out. Keep the fabric design folded.

MAKING THE TEMPLATE

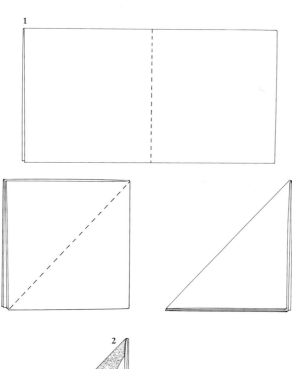

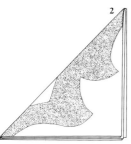

3

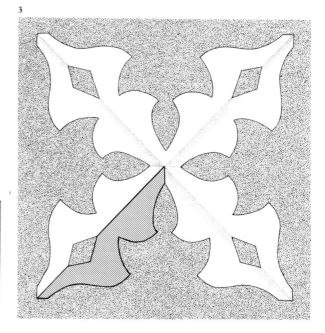

MARKING AND CUTTING

PREPARING TO SEW

SEWING

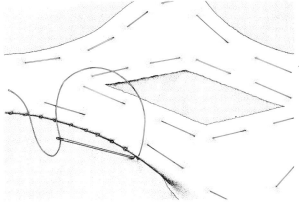

Use a thread as close as possible to the colour of the applied shape. Secure the shape to the background fabric with a small overcast stitch, using the side of the needle to roll the edges under 3mm ($\frac{1}{8}$in)

as you work. Continue until the appliqué is attached to the backing all the way round the outside and round any cut-out sections of the design. Remove the tacking stitches and press lightly.

PREPARING TO SEW

Take a square of background fabric large enough to accommodate the design plus a certain amount of space around the appliqué pattern and seam allowances. Fold it into eighths, following exactly the same order as before. Press lightly. Unfold the background fabric and lay it out right side up. Place the folded fabric shape on top and gradually unfold it, matching the folded lines to those of the background fabric. Working from the centre outwards, pin and tack it in position, keeping the stitches at least 12mm ($\frac{1}{2}$in) in from the edge, so that this can be turned under.

CONTOUR QUILTING

Quilting is an integral part of any Hawaiian appliqué design: it gives texture to the surface and shows up well against the plain fabrics used. The quilting is worked by hand, using a hoop or a frame, and the three layers are prepared in the usual way (see following chapter). Hawaiian appliqué is contour quilted, which means that the quilting echoes the shape of the applied piece. The quilting lines can be marked on the fabric or judged by the eye.

Traditionally, the stitching is worked in the same colour as the background and the lines of quilting are closely spaced, about 9 – 18mm ($\frac{3}{8}$ – $\frac{3}{4}$in) apart, depending on the size of the work. Begin in the centre and gradually work outwards.

The central theme of this contemporary Hawaiian quilt is a formalized design in red cotton appliquéd on to a white cotton background and representing Queen Kapiolani's fan and Kahilis – a native Hawaiian flower. All the motifs used in Hawaiian quilts are symbolic and recur frequently in different combinations. Traditionally, the different patterns were very closely associated with particular families and any encroachment would have been strongly resented. This quilt is backed in cotton and padded, and the red cotton border is also appliquéd. The rows of contour quilting are 12mm ($\frac{1}{2}$in) apart.

COMPLETING
THE TOP

When you have made enough blocks or have an area of patchwork large enough for your purpose, there are various ways of completing the work to give it a finished and unified appearance. Blocks can be joined together either straight or diagonally. If you are alternating pieced blocks with intricately quilted squares of plain fabric you might find it easier to use the quilt-as-you-go method (pp172–3). Patchwork or appliqué tops need not necessarily be quilted, however, and this section describes how to piece together a top formed from blocks which may or may not be alternated with lattice strips or plain squares and how to add border strips to frame the design. The resulting top might be quilted, but it could simply be backed and used as a decorative but cool coverlet, without wadding or quilting.

SETTING BLOCKS TOGETHER

The decision about whether to set blocks together, making a large overall pattern, or whether to separate them with plain strips or squares, throwing the emphasis on the individual blocks, will have been made at the design stage. When joining finished blocks, it is important to refer back to your original working drawing in order to check measurements (the completed blocks may vary slightly in size, but additional strips and squares must be cut to the design size). Whatever the design, the sewing procedure is the same: first sew units into rows, then sew rows together. In both cases, pin first at either end, then ease in any fullness or stretch slightly to fit, avoiding a difference in length at one end. To keep to the design size, sew pieced blocks to fit any plain blocks or lattice strips, rather than the other way round. Whether you are sewing by hand or machine, keep the side with most seams uppermost: this is particularly important when machine sewing, as it makes it easier to guide the seams under the presser foot.

Additional templates will be needed for plain squares and lattice strips. If half or quarter patchwork blocks are required to fill in at the edges, templates will also have to be specially made for these. Do not cut ordinary blocks, as there will be no seam allowances on the cut edges.

PIECED BLOCKS AND PLAIN SQUARES

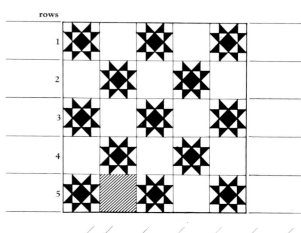

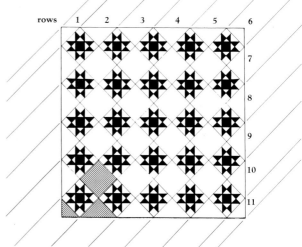

PIECED BLOCKS
AND PLAIN SQUARES
Pieced blocks can be set straight or diagonally, and alternated with squares of plain or patterned fabric, giving a chequered effect (the shaded areas represent additional templates needed). An odd number of blocks and rows are needed for a balanced design. The plain squares often have a quilted pattern, both for decorative effect and to prevent sagging, but if the quilting is minimal it is best to use a printed fabric to stop the squares looking empty.

When pieced blocks are set diagonally, either with plain squares or lattice strips, then they are joined together in diagonal rows. Start in either of the top corners (here, the top left corner) and make progressively longer rows until you reach the centre . Repeat for the other half of the top (starting from row 11 in the lower diagram), and then sew the two halves together.

LATTICE STRIPS

Lattice strips can be used to frame blocks, and if the latter are made from scraps of different fabrics, then the lattice effect creates a more harmonious pattern. The strips usually measure about a quarter of the length of a block in width and are generally cut to the length of a block, being linked by square intersections, as shown. (Long unwieldy strips would tend to stretch.) For a straight setting 1, make one template for the strip and one for the square intersection (see shaded areas). Additional quarter and half square intersections are needed for the edges of a diagonal setting 2 (plus the extra templates which will be required for the half blocks).

PIECED LATTICE STRIPS

Sometimes, instead of strips cut from plain or printed fabric, pieced strips can be used, forming an extension of the overall design. Make the additional templates and piece each strip together before joining rows.

ZIGZAG PATTERNS

Pieced blocks can be alternated with plain triangles and staggered, creating a horizontal or vertical zigzag effect. As well as the templates needed for the half blocks, two triangles are required: a large (half block) triangle and a smaller (quarter block) one, to complete the edges. To make each row, start by sewing a triangle to either side of a pieced block then join the row.

A quilt using the Variable Star pattern set diagonally with lattice strips and a sawtooth edging (top of picture). Quarter and half blocks are needed to fill the edges.

LATTICE STRIPS **1**

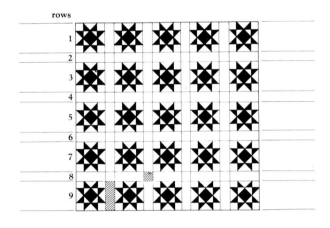

PIECED LATTICE STRIPS

2

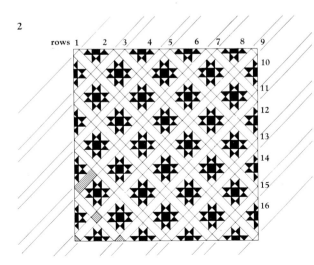

ZIGZAG PATTERNS

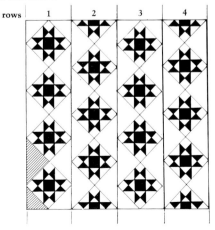

BORDERS

Well-proportioned borders make a satisfying frame to contain the different elements in a pieced or appliqué quilt. They also offer a way of making the quilt up to the required size, but in either case the border must be seen as part of the whole quilt and planned at the outset, not only for estimating fabric, but so that it forms part of the design. Unplanned borders look like an afterthought.

Cut the border strips to the size specified in the original design and fit the patchwork to the border rather than the other way round. This will ensure that the border strips lie flat and are all the correct size. Most borders are joined with straight seams at the corners, or have a separate corner square or just a mitred seam. If you are being economical and using several lengths of fabric instead of a long strip, it looks much neater if the seams are aligned with those of the patchwork or appliqué. Borders can be attached by hand, but it is quicker to use a machine, even if the main work is hand sewn.

Lay the work out flat when attaching borders, and mark and pin the border strips at points corresponding to the main pattern, so that the border fits evenly. For example, if a patchwork top is composed of blocks measuring 22.5cm (9in), then the border can be marked every 22.5cm and aligned with the blocks.

STRAIGHT BORDERS

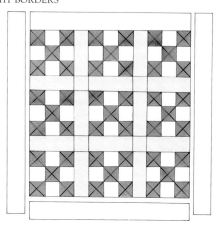

Using the measurements given on your original design, cut two strips to the finished width of the patchwork or appliqué top, adding a seam allowance all round. Attach these to the top and bottom of the work. Again referring to the original design, make two side strips to the finished length of the patchwork plus the finished width of the border strip at either end, adding seam allowances all round. Finish by attaching the side strips.

CORNER SQUARES

Using the design measurements, plus seam allowances, cut two strips to the length of the patchwork and two to the width. Make four squares to the width of the finished border, plus seam allowances. Join the squares to either end of the side strips and then attach the border strips as for straight borders.

MITRED CORNERS

Cut the two side strips to the same length as the completed top plus two border widths and repeat this for both the top and bottom strips. Attach the strips as for straight borders but leave the ends free. Lap the side ends over the top and bottom ends, then make a diagonal fold at each corner, from the corner of the patchwork to the outer corner of the border. At each corner, hand sew the top fabric to the layer underneath, stitching along the folded edge and using a running or blind stitch. This method works best on wide borders: for narrower ones, make mitred corners by the method shown opposite.

corner detail

BACKING

A patchwork or appliqué top is not always quilted. Some designs do not call for a raised textured effect, and sometimes the warmth of wadding is not needed. However, it still requires a backing, both to neaten the work and to strengthen it. Select fabric of a similar weight to those used for the top. If you are making a full-sized cover, you will have to join several widths of fabric to make a piece the same size as the top. Tie the two layers together (pp176–7) to prevent the backing from sagging and distorting the top.

EASY BACKING METHOD

EASY BACKING METHOD
The simplest way of adding a backing is to cut a piece of fabric the same size as the top, including seam allowances. Place the top and backing right sides together, then pin

and stitch round all the edges, leaving the middle third of one edge open. Trim the corners as shown, turn the work right side out and slip stitch to close.

SELF-BINDING EDGE
A self-binding edge can be made by simply bringing the edge of the backing fabric over to the front or taking the front edge back. The backing will need to be larger than the top for the former, vice-versa for the latter. Stitch top and bottom edges first, then the sides. Fold the corners with a straight seam 1, or, for a neater effect, mitre them 2.

In this quilt, which she has titled 'Reds under the Bed', Iona Heath has emphasized the corners by making large, separate, nine-patch blocks, which are in sympathy with the main design but different from it. The plain black border strips are quilted with strongly functional stitches, making a diamond pattern.

SELF-BINDING EDGE
1 straight corner

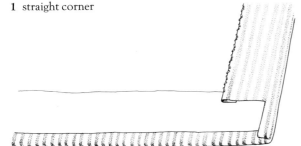

2 mitred corner

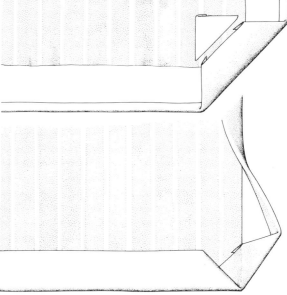

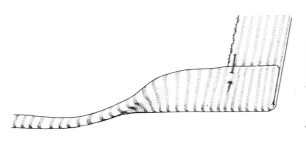

Deirdre Amsden working at a quilting frame in her studio, which is a converted chapel.

4. QUILTING

A close inspection of a quilt reveals a linear pattern made by small running stitches: these have a decorative purpose but they hold together the three layers – the top, the backing and the middle layer of wadding, without which it would be a coverlet instead of a quilt. In whole cloth quilts the stitching is the only means of decoration, but within this is an area rich in interpretation: the surface is softly sculptured, appealing to both the visual and tactile senses, and the patterns formed by the lines of stitching are emphasized by a subtle play of light and shade.

On traditional quilts, patterns can be categorized as single motifs, filler patterns and border designs. Patchwork quilts made for everyday use might have individual patches outlined with quilting or might be quilted all over in simple grid designs. More elaborate quilting was to be found on 'best' quilts, and if a quilter really wanted to show off her stitches as well as her pieced work, patchwork blocks were alternated with plain squares elaborately worked. Good quilting was and still is much admired.

The techniques used to make patterns and templates for traditional quilting patterns can be applied to contemporary designs. Most quiltmakers are introduced to quilting via traditional patterns made by the folding paper method, but more individual designs can be invented. Inspiration can be drawn from everyday things, as Deirdre Amsden has done with her footprint quilts. If a patchwork or appliqué top is being quilted, the stitching can do much more than simply echo the shapes: as an individual element within the overall design, it can complement the fabric shapes but remain distinct from them.

Whether the pattern is traditional or modern, contrast of scale within an overall design gives it added interest and texture. Heavily quilted work recedes whereas openly worked areas come forward; the closer the lines, the more dense is the texture created by the quilting. Hand quilting is totally different from machine quilting, which has a unique character well suited to contemporary designs and to heavier fabrics, which are more difficult to sew by hand. Italian and trapunto quilting, which can be sewn by hand or machine, were developed for their attractive decorative effect rather than for warmth. If you like working in small units, try the quilt-as-you-go technique, which simplifies the quilting of a large area by dividing it into sections. If you have no time at all to quilt, you can simply button or tuft the layers.

QUILTING EQUIPMENT

Most of the sewing equipment mentioned in the previous chapter is also needed for quilting, plus a few additional items for more specialized techniques. Marking equipment is listed on p164.

Hoop or frame Use one or the other to keep the layers evenly stretched during hand quilting (see pp166–9).

Tapes Two lengths of 2.5cm (1in) wide plain tape are pinned to the edges of the quilt to hold it in a frame.

Thimbles For hand quilting, use a thimble (make sure that you have a comfortable fit) on the middle finger of your sewing hand. This is needed to guide the needle through the layers, enabling several stitches to be taken at once.

Needles For hand quilting, a good supply of short fine needles is required. Use 8 or 9 betweens (the higher the number the smaller the needle). For machine quilting, match the needle to the fabric and thread. A chenille needle is used for buttoning, and a long, round-headed bodkin for Italian quilting.

Crochet hook This is used to insert the stuffing in trapunto work.

FABRICS

Top and backing fabrics The top and backing fabrics should be similar in weight and both should be prewashed to remove any dressing, making them softer and easier to quilt. In general, fabrics made from natural fibres are most suitable for hand quilting and it is also important to choose fabrics which are easy to pierce with a needle (which is why closely woven sheeting is not always suitable for a backing).

The easiest fabrics to sew are pure dressweight cottons. Fine linen, silk, satin and lawn, or wool and cotton mixtures such as Viyella are also suitable. More resilient man-made fibres can be used in machine work, but avoid fabrics that feel too rigid and lack the give needed to create the raised, quilted effect. Lustrous fabrics such as silk and satin give a richer appearance than plain cottons, and light colours reflect the highlights and contrast with the shadows better than dark ones. Plain fabrics show up the stitches, but some prints suggest quilting designs and beginners may prefer to choose a printed backing fabric to conceal any unevenness. Alternatively, a top-quality unbleached calico is often a good choice for a backing fabric.

WADDING

A filling or wadding is required to give a relief effect to the quilting patterns. The type of wadding used will affect the appearance of the quilt, and your choice will be influenced by this, by the end use of the quilt, and by whether it is to be laundered or dry cleaned.

Traditionally, quilts were filled with carded fleece, but few quiltmakers now have access to fleece or time for its preparation. The most commonly used wadding today is the washable polyester type. Choose a bonded wadding, in which the fibres are bonded together to prevent them from creeping through the top fabric, an effect which is known as bearding and is particularly noticeable on darker colours. Synthetic wadding is available in several thicknesses: the thinnest, 56g (2oz), grade is the least springy and therefore the easiest to sew by hand or machine. The thicker the wadding, the more difficult it will be to make small stitches, and the thickest type is best reserved for the buttoning and tufting techniques. Synthetic wadding has the advantage of requiring less quilting than other types. Before use, it is best to unfold it and lay it flat, allowing it to regain its body.

Alternatives to polyester include dense cotton wadding, which is used fluffy side up. This needs closer lines of quilting and produces a flatter effect, but it is ideal for machine work and gives additional weight, which makes a quilt hang well. If the quilting is closely worked the item can be washed, but dry cleaning is advisable if it is less densely quilted.

Domett also gives a flatter appearance than synthetic wadding and is better dry cleaned. The woollen type has an open knitted, fluffy texture and is less suitable than the cotton, which is similar to flannelette sheeting but shrinks when washed. Thin blankets can also be used for filling and combine weight with warmth, but again give a flat appearance and are more difficult to quilt.

The raised look of a quilt can be spoiled by ironing. Synthetic waddings, in particular, will be reduced to paper thickness, even by an iron that is only warm. However, most wrinkles can be smoothed out by hand (and will tend to be removed by the effect of the quilting).

Italian, trapunto, and shadow quilting The top fabrics listed for ordinary quilting are also suitable for Italian and trapunto work. Transparent fabrics such as organza, voile or fine silk are used for shadow quilting, where the colour of the filling intentionally shows through. Mull – a thin, plain cotton muslin – is ideal as a backing for this type of work, since the threads can be teased open without breaking to allow the stuffing to be inserted. Cotton lawn is suitable, but in this case small cuts must be made. For Italian quilting, use special quilting wool to make the smooth lines. Kapok or loose synthetic wadding is used for trapunto work.

Joining fabrics It is often necessary to join lengths of fabric and wadding to make a full-size quilt. If top or backing fabrics must be joined, avoid centre seams. Use a complete width of fabric for the centre and half widths at either side. Seams are generally organized to run down the length of a quilt and are kept symmetrical, to produce a well-balanced appearance.

If strips of wadding have to be joined, butt the edges against each other and join them with a herringbone stitch. This avoids making a ridge which would show on the surface.

THREAD

Use a pure cotton No. 40 wrapped polyester or a special quilting thread. For hand sewing, always knot the end you cut and run the thread through beeswax to strengthen it and prevent tangling. Use silk thread for silk fabrics. The colour can be selected either to match or to contrast with that of the top fabric. Use a cheaper fine cotton thread for tacking the layers together.

A thicker thread is needed for buttoning and tufting. It will also hold the reef knot but only if the thread is pure cotton.

QUILTING TEMPLATES

Quilting templates can be bought, but they are also easy to make. Basically, they consist of outlines which can be filled in with additional details; for example, a leaf shape with veins. In the case of home-made templates, these details are drawn in by hand, but bought templates are generally stencils, with the internal lines indicated by long dashes. Whichever form they take, the templates can be used either to draw the pattern directly on the top fabric or to make a paper design which is then transferred to the fabric (see p164).

Traditional quilting motifs were generally based on everyday objects such as cups, glasses, flowers and feathers, and patterns were handed down from generation to generation. The shapes can be realistic or geometric, used singly or repeated, and the methods used to make the traditional patterns can easily be adapted for contemporary work.

Designs for templates can be drawn on paper, stuck to card and then cut out, using the same basic method as for patchwork templates (see pp132-3), or you can make them from folded paper cut-outs, as shown here. When the template outlines have been drawn, any internal quilting lines can be drawn in either in continuous lines or, as here, with dotted lines.

EQUIPMENT

Much of the equipment needed for quilting templates is the same as that used for patchwork templates (p132): compasses, fine lead pencil, spray adhesive, metal ruler, set square and craft knife. You will also need the following:

Paper Use lightweight paper for the folding and cutting method shown here, or slightly heavier paper for templates.

Card Use postcard-weight card for paper motifs, and heavier card for repeated shapes.

Scissors Paper cutting scissors are needed to cut out the paper motifs. Many card templates are easily cut with a craft knife, but use a pair of curved surgical scissors for small rounded shapes.

TEMPLATES BASED ON A CIRCLE

Many attractive quilting patterns can be made from templates based on a circle. Remove the centre section so that the quilting lines do not all meet at the centre and create a muddled pattern. Circles can be drawn with a pair of compasses or a plate or glass. Use lightweight paper which will fold easily and produce accurate divisions. When the paper shapes are made, they can then be stuck to card and cut out. Inside details can be filled in either freehand or with ruled lines.

1 A rose pattern can be made from a circle folded into eight and cut to produce petals. The divisions between petals can be indicated by curves.

2 Another rose pattern can be made in the same way, folding the paper into 16 sections.

3 Hearts can be made from a quarter of an eight-petal rose, and can be used on their own or adapted and repeated, **5**.

4 A quarter of a 16-petal rose makes a fan for a corner.

6 Stars can be made from circles folded into 16 sections.

TEMPLATES BASED ON A CIRCLE

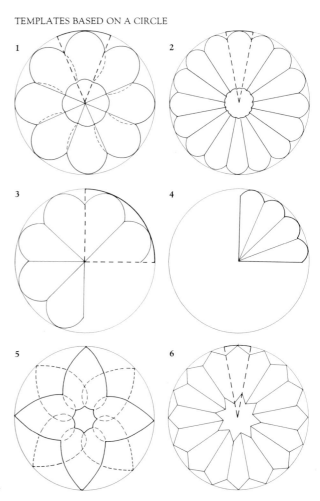

TEAR-BASED MOTIFS

REPEATED SHAPES

A repeated template shape forms the basis of motifs, borders and filler patterns. If you are using a template to make a regular pattern repeat, mark the edges with a dot or notch where they intersect with adjoining shapes so that they are easy to position accurately.

TEAR-BASED MOTIFS
Many intricate quilting patterns are based on a simple tear shape. Make the tear template on p184 to the size you require. Position the tear at regularly marked intervals: between two parallel straight or wavy lines for a border, between concentric circles for a wreath. For freer forms like leaves and feathers, overlap the tear template within a roughly drawn outline.

BORDER AND FILLER PATTERNS

BORDER AND FILLER PATTERNS
Mark the limits of the pattern area on the top fabric, making sure that lines enclosing a border are parallel and using a large set square to ensure that corners are at right angles. Mark the centre point on each side of a square template, and make four equidistant marks on the edge of a circular template. Position the first template symmetrically at the corner of the pattern area and draw round it. Mark in the dots as shown. Move the template along, using the dots to give the correct alignment, and repeat. Continue along the border or over the surface. Fill in any internal quilting lines with a ruler.

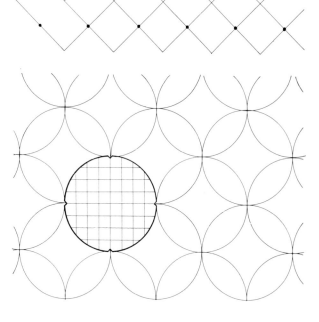

How a professional arranges a complex pattern: in this quilt by Mrs Emms (see also pp 92–3), the running feather and cable patterns are subtly elongated to curve elegantly round the corner. A diagonal grid of quilting fills the spaces between the central figure and border motifs.

MARKING QUILTING PATTERNS

Quilters used to mark the pattern as the work progressed and after it had been put in the frame, but unless you are very experienced it is easier to mark out the complete pattern before the three layers have been put together. Mark the pattern on the right side of the top fabric, after dividing it into quarters by pressing it lightly or using tacking stitches to make a useful grid. If you are marking with a needle or a coloured pencil, lay the fabric over a piece of flannelette or a similarly thick material. Do not use lead pencils, felt tips or biros, which are messy and spoil the finished work, or tailor's chalk, as it makes a thick line.

EQUIPMENT

Once the templates have been prepared, there are several different ways of marking out a quilting pattern, and the equipment needed will depend on the method chosen.

Coloured pencils One of the most straightforward methods is to draw round the templates with a well sharpened pencil in a colour close to that of the top fabric. If the design is drawn lightly, it will usually disappear during quilting or can be brushed off at the finish.

Tracing method For this method, in addition to the templates and a black felt tip pen, you will need a sheet of paper the size of the design, a black coloured pencil and masking tape. The method can only be used with light coloured, relatively fine fabrics, through which the lines will show: mark the complete design on paper, using a black felt tip pen, then place the fabric right side up on top of the paper pattern and, as with the previous method, draw on the fabric with a coloured pencil. The design and the fabric should be held in position with masking tape.

Dressmaker's carbon This can be obtained from most good haberdashery shops. The design should first be drawn on tracing paper, which is then pinned or taped to the top fabric with the carbon paper (carbon side down) in between. Trace over the design lines with a hard lead pencil or a tracing wheel.

Perforated patterns Draw the design on paper, then machine stitch along the lines with an unthreaded needle to create a perforated pattern. Position the design right side-up on the right side of the fabric and tape it in place. Gently rub French chalk or pounce over the surface to produce a dotted chalk outline. Remove the pattern and go over the lines with a coloured pencil. This method is time consuming and is not necessary for simple designs but it is useful for complicated patterns.

Masking tape Although this method is suitable only for straight lines, it is quick and easy and can be done when the work is already in the hoop or frame. Position the tape so that one edge marks the quilting line and stitch along that edge. The tape can then be peeled off and reused for the next line. Use masking tape only, as this can easily be peeled off and will not leave sticky marks on the fabric.

Rug needle A simple but effective method of marking, shown below; only the templates and a blunt-ended rug needle are required.

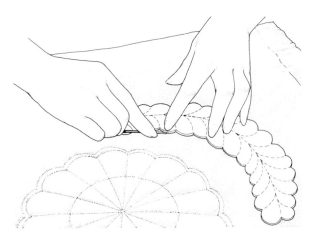

NEEDLE MARKING
This is the traditional method of marking quilting patterns and works best with natural fibres. Lay the top fabric, right side up, on a piece of flannelette; hold the needle against the template, at an angle almost parallel to the fabric, and press down. Follow the edge of the template, marking a fine indented line, which will remain until the work is completed. If you make a mistake the line can be removed by slightly damping the fabric and lightly pressing with a warm iron.

HAND QUILTING

THE QUILTING STITCH

Hand quilting is worked with a small, evenly spaced running stitch, which joins the three layers together. As you become used to quilting, a pleasant, relaxing rhythm is established and the stitches naturally become more even and easier to sew. Ideally they should be about 2mm ($\frac{1}{10}$in) long, but evenness of stitching and regular spacing are more important to the overall appearance of the work. In any case, the length of the stitches will be affected by the thickness of the wadding, and if it is very thick or the seams of a patchwork top make quilting difficult, it may be easier to abandon the running stitch at times and work with a stab stitch, bringing the needle up and down through the layers in separate movements.

Use a No. 8 quilting needle and No. 40 sewing cotton or a special quilting thread (first passed through beeswax so it runs smoothly through the layers). Where possible, sew in continuous lines, following the natural flow of the pattern. Whether working with a hoop or with a frame, complete one section before moving on to the next. In each section, work the main shapes first and then the filler patterns. To work the lines as continuous rows of stitching, keep several needles in action and progress evenly across the surface of the quilt. The stitches should be firm but not so tight as to pucker the fabric.

This centre detail is from a whole cloth quilt made in the North of England in the 1920s or 1930s. It shows a good interaction of quilting styles: the large rose within an eight-pointed star and the surrounding whorls (normally associated with Wales).

THE RUNNING STITCH

Use about 40cm (16in) of thread, with a knot at the cut end, and push the needle up from the back to the starting point of the sewing line, pulling the thread so that the knot goes through the backing fabric and anchors itself in the wadding. Work with a thimble on the middle finger of your sewing hand, using it to guide the needle through all three layers. Keep your other hand under the work to check that the needle has passed through all the layers and to guide it back up again. At first, take one stitch at a time, but aim to increase this to four to six stitches, as this will help to keep the stitches more even. The thumb of the sewing hand should be extended, pressing down the material just ahead of the point of the needle as it comes to the top.

To finish, make a knot close to the last stitch; take the thread through to the back, and again anchor the knot in the wadding, trimming the end. Alternatively, you can make a back stitch, splitting the previous stitch, and then lose the end of the thread in the wadding.

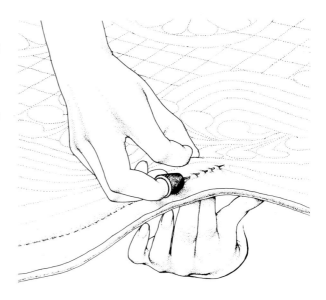

USING A HOOP

People working in a restricted space often prefer to use a hoop rather than a frame. Quilting hoops, like embroidery hoops, hold the work taut between the inner ring and an outer one which is tightened with a screw. They range from 45cm (18in) up to 60cm (24in) in diameter. The largest size allows a larger area to be quilted at one time. Some hoops have a stand, which leaves both hands free to stitch, while others must be rested against the edge of a table.

One advantage of using a hoop is that the work can be turned so that you can stitch in different directions, which cannot be done with a frame. A disadvantage is that more extensive preparation by tacking is needed, and the work receives more handling. Don't leave the work in the hoop for any length of time – even overnight – as this can mark the fabric permanently.

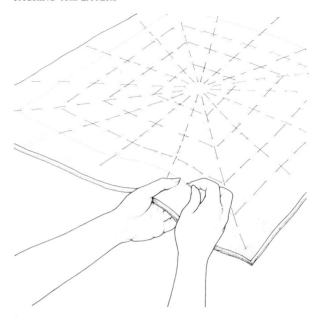

TACKING THE LAYERS
Cut the three layers to the same size, allowing several inches on all sides for neatening and because the quilting process tends to reduce the overall size. Assemble the layers on a flat surface: backing wrong side up, wadding, and finally the marked top fabric, right side up. Tape the corners to prevent the layers shifting. Smooth out wrinkles and lightly pin the layers together, working from centre to corners. Tacking knots at the centre can hide the pattern, so take a good length of thread and work out to one corner, leaving a long tail at the centre. Rethread the needle with the tail end and work out to the other corner. Tack to all corners then to equally spaced points in between. Return to the centre and tack in a series of concentric squares 7 to 15cm (3 to 6in) apart. Tack round the edges to finish.

LARGE AREAS
When handling large areas, the best method is to assemble the layers in stages.

1 Take the backing fabric and fold it into quarters, wrong side inside, then mark the centre point on each edge with a pin, placed horizontally on the fold line. Working on a flat surface, carefully unfold the fabric, wrong side up. If necessary, tape each corner down to hold it in position.

2 Mark the centre point on each outside edge of the wadding, as for the backing. Fold the wadding in half and place it on top of the backing fabric so that the folded edge aligns with the pins which mark the centre points of the backing fabric. Gently turn back the fold so that the wadding lies flat and the pins match.

3 Fold the marked top in quarters, with the marked side inside, and pin the centre of each edge, as before. Place the folded top in one corner of the two prepared layers, aligning corresponding pins, and carefully unfold it, smoothing out wrinkles with a metre rule. Pin and tack as usual.

If it is difficult to reach the centre point in order to tack, carefully roll up one half of the quilt and work on the flat half, then repeat the process for the other side.

WORKING WITH LARGE AREAS

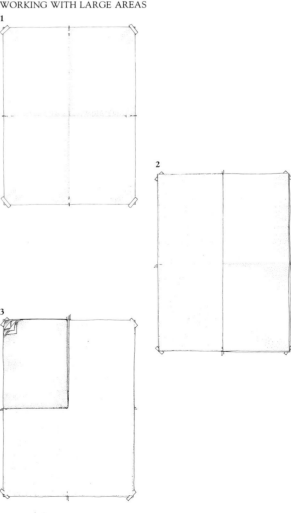

SETTING THE QUILT IN THE HOOP

Always start quilting in the centre of the work and progress evenly outwards. Place the inner hoop under the central area of the tacked work. Smooth out the work, then loosen the outer hoop and slide it in place over the work and the inner hoop. Tighten the outer hoop so that the layers are evenly stretched and are smooth on both sides (always remember to check the back of the work). The layers should be held firmly in the hoop, but there should be enough give to allow several stitches to be taken on at one time. As each area of quilting is completed, move the hoop to a new section. Remove tacking when the entire work is complete.

QUILTING THE EDGES

When working round the edges of a quilt or at a corner it is important that the work is still held in the hoop or the edges will be pulled out of true. To achieve this, add strips of fabric to the edges so that they can be fitted into the hoop: cut two lengths of fabric, for example old sheeting, 15cm (6in) wide, and fold under a 2.5cm (1in) seam down each strip. Position the folded edges to overlap along the edge of the quilt, then tack the strips in position so that they cross at the corner. Put the work in the hoop as before. The same method can also be used for small pieces of work, such as blocks, which could not be quilted in a frame.

QUILTING THE EDGES

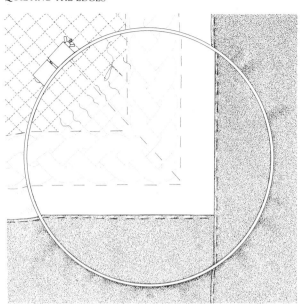

SETTING THE QUILT IN THE HOOP

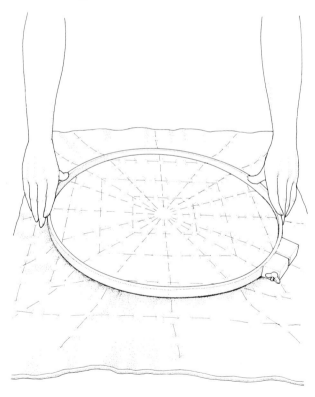

In 'Nine Fold Harmony', Dawn Pavitt manipulates the Diamond Log Cabin technique to create a visually pleasing design made up from nine large eight-pointed stars, all set against an elaborately quilted and luminous blue ground. Each of the individual diamond blocks follows the same graded light-to-dark colour sequence around the central diamond until the last round of strips. The sequence is then changed to avoid an overpowering image at the centre and a harsh continuous line round the outer edge. The quilting casts the background into relief, creating a textured area of circular feather patterns with star motifs, and the quilt is framed by a cable border.

USING A FRAME

In the past, large quilts were almost always worked on a frame. They were cumbersome and when not in use might be hoisted up to the ceiling. Alternatively, the front room or parlour was sometimes set aside for quilting so that the work could be left undisturbed. Lack of space is the main reason why frames are less popular today, but they still have several advantages over hoops. For one thing, the work requires less tacking, and for another, it can be left set up over a longer period, so the fabric receives less handling. In addition, the quilt can be stitched as a continuous piece, right up to the edge, and last but not least, if you enjoy working with other people, a frame enables several people to work together on a single quilt.

If you are buying a frame, note that the measurement given is for the length of the webbing (see below), and the frame itself will often be longer. Frames can be taken apart for storage, and if you like using them it is best to have both a large and a small one.

A QUILTING FRAME

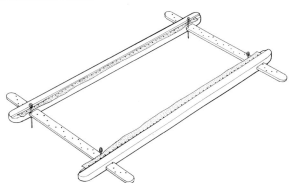

SETTING UP THE FRAME

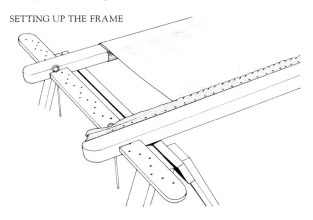

A QUILTING FRAME
This consists of two long bars, the runners, and two shorter cross pieces, the stretchers, which fit through slots in the bars and are held in place by pegs or small clamps. Webbing, on which to sew the backing fabric, is attached to one edge of each runner. The webbing must be long enough to accommodate either the full length or the width of the quilt. Mark the centre point of the webbing to align it with the centre of the quilt.

SETTING UP THE FRAME
Cut the backing fabric so that all the sides align with the straight or cross grain. Lay the runners parallel to each other on a table. Mark the centre on the bottom edge of the backing fabric and turn under a 12mm (½in) seam, then match it with the marked centre on the webbing of the bottom runner (the one nearest to you). Oversew the backing to the webbing, working outwards from the centre in each

direction. Attach the top edge of the fabric to the top runner, then roll the surplus fabric on the top runner, leaving about 45cm (18in) exposed. Secure the stretchers in place with pegs or clamps. There should be enough give in the fabric to enable several stitches to be taken at one time.

WADDING AND TOP FABRIC
Spread the wadding over the backing fabric, aligning the sides and bottom and letting the surplus hang over the top runner. Smooth it flat. Position the top fabric in the same way. Smooth the layers flat, then tack the wadding and top fabric to the webbing of the bottom runner, making sure that the stitches go through the webbing. Using quilting needles, pin the layers together in a line parallel to the top runner and about 5cm (2in) below it. The layers draped over the top runner can be pinned up or protected with an old sheet to prevent them from sweeping the floor.

WADDING

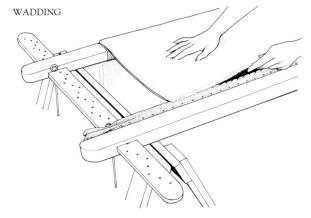

TOP FABRIC

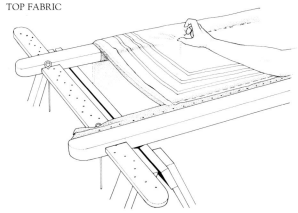

SECURING AND
MOVING THE WORK

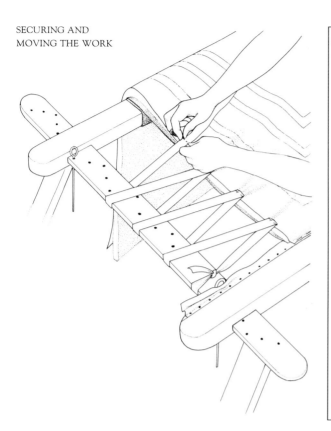

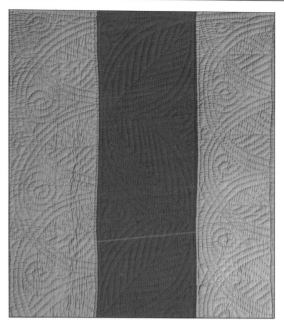

Plain strippy quilts were assembled in the frame with the strips parallel to the webbing and marked as the work progressed. This Welsh strippy shows the traditional flat leaves, semi-circles and spirals.

SECURING AND
MOVING THE WORK
Take a length of tape 2.5cm (1in) wide and tie it round one of the stretchers, close to the bottom runner. Attach the tape with a needle to the three layers, then take it over and back under the stretcher and attach it to the three layers as before. Continue in this way, attaching the tape to the layers at about 7.5cm (3in) intervals along one side. Repeat for the other side. Work the quilting evenly, stitching from right to left (if right handed) and from the bottom edge up towards the top runner. When the exposed area has been quilted, remove the needles holding the side tapes and, holding the work steady at the far end, take out the pegs and remove the stretchers. Unroll some more backing fabric from the top runner and carefully roll the completed work round the bottom runner. Set up the work as before, making sure that you can continue the quilting where it has been left off.

TAPESTRY FRAMES

A tapestry frame is useful for making small pieces of work or for quilting individual units, but it is much smaller than even a small-size quilting frame. It is, however, a good way of finding out whether you prefer quilting with a frame instead of a hoop: the setting-up procedure is slightly different, but the basic sewing method is much the same as for a larger frame.

USING A TAPESTRY FRAME

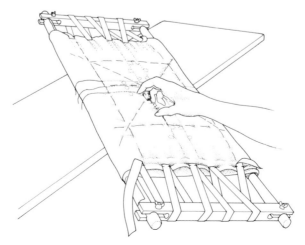

USING A TAPESTRY FRAME
If you are working on a small, tapestry-type frame, the setting-up procedure is slightly different from that used for a normal quilting frame. Assemble the three layers together (backing fabric wrong side up, wadding, then marked top fabric right side up) and lightly tack them. Sew the top and bottom ends of the work to the top and bottom rails of the frame, tacking through all three layers, then roll any surplus equally round each roller to expose the centre. Add the stretchers and tape the sides. When sewing, rest the frame against a table, leaving the hands free. As the work progresses, roll on a new area until you have quilted one half of the work, then go back to the centre and repeat the process for the other half. On a small piece of work, you can snip the tacking stitches if they get in the way of the quilting stitches, and you can also leave thread ends instead of needles as you work across.

MACHINE QUILTING

Machine quilting has its own distinctive character and a contemporary feel: don't think of it as a substitute for hand quilting, but exploit its qualities for their own sake. Its hard-lined appearance is particularly suited to non-traditional quilting designs based on geometrical shapes and grids of straight lines. Machining is impractical for tight, intricate curves, and its hard lines also conflict visually with many traditional patchwork and appliqué patterns. The best solution for combining machine quilting with traditional patterns is to use sink stitching.

Although machine quilting is quicker than hand quilting, and the stitches are stronger, it needs plenty of time and preparation for a successful result. Before starting, make sure your machine is operating smoothly, the bobbin is full and the needle sharp. Work on a large table so that the quilt does not slip off and pull away from the machine. Even single size quilts are difficult to feed through a machine, so if possible use the quilt-as-you-go method (see pp172–3), and work in smaller units; dividing the quilt, for example, into halves, quarters, or small groups of blocks.

MARKING AND TACKING
Mark out the pattern on the top fabric before putting the layers together. If you are using a quilting foot, simply divide the area into quarters with two lines, either running straight (for a square grid) or diagonally (for diamonds). The presser foot can be used as a guide when making lines of quilting 6mm (¼in) apart, but it is still necessary to mark the main guide lines.

It is vital that the backing fabric lies flat while the work is being fed through the machine. On small units, it is sufficient to tack through the three layers, but on larger units double tacking is advisable. Begin by laying the wadding flat on a hard surface and taping it down at the corners, taking care not to stretch it.

1 *Lay the backing on top, right side up, and again tape it at the corners. Tack the two together in the usual way (see p166).*

2 *Remove the tape and turn over the layers so that the wadding is on top. Tape the corners again.*

3 *Position the top fabric, right side up, over the wadding and tape the corners. Tack, keeping slightly away from the marked pattern and making*

MARKING AND TACKING

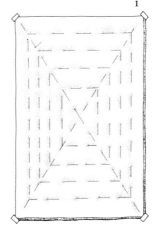

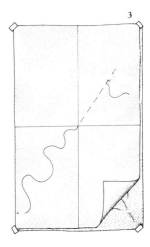

sure that the stitches are not so big that they will get caught round the presser foot. This top tacking can be removed as the quilting progresses.

TACKING WITH PINS
This is a useful alternative to tacking with thread, and avoids the nuisance caused by tangled tacking and quilting threads. There is a danger of being pricked, but the pins can be removed as the work progresses. (They will be easier to remove if they are placed so that the pointed ends will face towards the presser foot.) Pin the layers together, keeping the pins parallel to the quilting lines but not so close to them that they might jam under the presser foot.

TACKING WITH PINS

SEWING

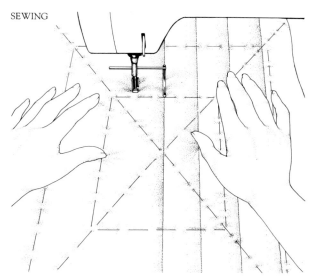

SINK STITCHING
Sink stitches can only be seen on the underside of the work; they are invisible on the right side. Tack or pin the layers together: pinning helps to hold the seam open. Place the pins in the seams, with the points facing towards the presser foot: they can easily be removed before the needle goes over them. Start at one end and, where possible, try always to work in the same direction. Hold the work flat, but at the same time try to open up the seams as much as possible, so that when the slight tension is released, the stitches sink into the seam line and are hidden.

REMOVING STITCHES
To remove an unwanted line of stitches, clip about every fourth stitch on the top side of the work and cover the line with masking tape. Pull out the bottom thread and remove the tape from the top. The tape will easily pull away the unwanted stitches.

SEWING
Use a slightly longer stitch than for normal machining and loosen the tension. Set the machine to a straight stitch and do not begin or end with a back stitch. Keep the work flat with your hands, but at the same time avoid pushing the layers so that they shift and become uneven at the edges.

Choose one edge as the top edge of the work and try to stitch all new rows in the same direction to prevent the fabric from puckering. Stitch in parallel lines from the centre line outwards towards one edge, then return to the centre and work the second half. When all the lines running in one direction have been stitched, turn the work through 90 degrees and work the crosswise rows beginning from the centre line.

Using a quilting foot saves marking every stitching line.

Simply adjust the bar to the width required between the lines of stitching. At the top edge, align the end of the bar with the centre line and stitch, keeping parallel to it. Start the next line again at the top edge, this time aligning the bar with the previous line of stitching.

Stitch one half of the quilt and then the other half, as already described .

FINISHING THE ENDS
Pull all thread ends through to the back of the work. Where quilting lines run from edge to edge, simply trim the ends: they will be secured by the final edging or binding. Where lines begin in the middle of the work, knot each pair of ends, thread them through a large needle and pull them through into the wadding.

SINK STITCHING

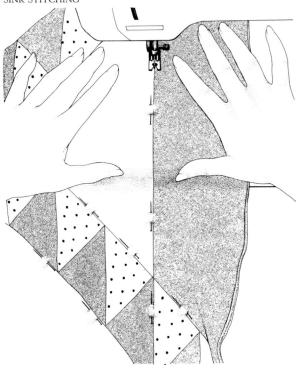

FINISHING THE ENDS

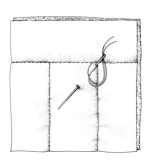

REMOVING STITCHES

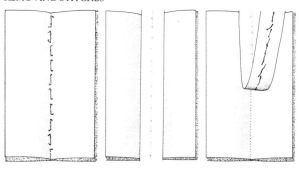

QUILT-AS-YOU-GO

Not everyone wants to embark on a full-size quilt whose bulk can be difficult to stitch, particularly if you want to make a closely set pattern by machine. The quilt-as-you-go technique neatly solves this problem by dividing a large quilt into more manageable units which can then be quilted by hand or machine. Although it is ideally suited to quilts formed from repeated patchwork or appliqué blocks, it is a good way of working the quilting for any design which can be separated into smaller working units. Basically, the individual units are quilted and are then sewn together, a tape or a strip of backing fabric being used to cover the seams. No additional lining is required, though you may prefer to add a backing to cover the strips at the back, securing it with buttons or tufts (p177).

The crazy quilt-as-you-go technique is a further development, in which the patchwork and quilting are machine sewn in one action. This is an excellent way of making a quilt quickly and using up oddments of fabric, and could be adapted to other patterns such as Log Cabin blocks.

For either method, use 56g (2oz) synthetic or cotton wadding, or cotton domett.

BASIC QUILT-AS-YOU-GO

In basic quilt-as-you-go, the patchwork or appliqué is sewn before the blocks are quilted, and effectively it is like making miniature quilts in the normal way and then joining them into one big piece, whereas in crazy quilt-as-you-go the patchwork is formed as the block is quilted.

PREPARING THE UNITS

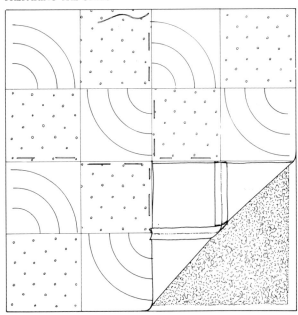

Before blocks are joined together, start by drawing the quilting pattern on the top fabric of each block in the usual way, but making sure that the design does not continue over the seam line on the outside edges. (If you are joining patchwork or appliqué blocks, the quilting might simply take the form of sink stitching, see pp170–1.) For each unit, cut backing fabric to the same size as the top and wadding to the same size but without the seam allowances.

QUILTING

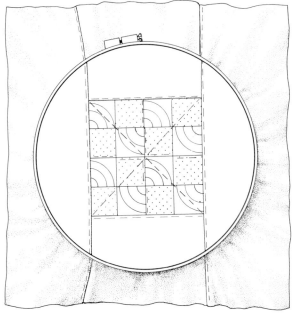

Assemble the three layers together, making sure that the wadding is positioned correctly. Pin at each corner, then tack, avoiding the quilting pattern as much as possible. Tack thoroughly and handle the work gently, so that the wadding does not shift during quilting. For hand quilting, use a hoop, even for small pieces. Tack four overlapping lengths of fabric to the sides of the unit if necessary, so that the work can be held in the hoop (see p167). Work the quilting pattern. Repeat for each individual unit. Join blocks and rows together, using the crazy quilt-as-you-go technique.

CRAZY QUILT-AS-YOU-GO

Crazy quilt-as-you-go is an excellent method to use for rag-bag projects: tiny scraps can be incorporated, and because they are stitched to a foundation they can even vary slightly in weight. You will also need a backing fabric and wadding; 2.5cm (1in) tape; a square template made to the finished size plus a 6mm ($\frac{1}{4}$in) seam allowance all round, and a second template, cut about 2cm ($\frac{3}{4}$in) larger all round. Before starting to sew, iron the patchwork fabrics (if they are from a rag-bag) and cut them into patches of random sizes.

In 'Banana Split' (see also pp50–51), the individual blocks were pieced, then each one was laid on a square of cotton domett and machine quilted.

STARTING A BLOCK
With the larger template, cut squares from backing fabric and wadding. Take a piece of backing fabric, wrong side up, and place a piece of wadding on top. Pin at each corner. Take a patch and pin it, right side up, to the centre of the square. Take a second patch and place it on top of the first, right sides together, aligning the two patches down one edge. The edge of the second patch must be long enough to cover the first. Pin and sew the patches together through all layers. At the end of each line, pull the threads to the top, knot the ends and trim them (backstitching would show on the reverse of the work).

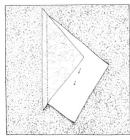

ADDING PATCHES
Turn the second patch right side up and pin it. Take a third patch and align it, right sides together, along the next edge of the centre patch, covering the end of the second patch. Pin and stitch it, then turn it back, right side up, and pin it in position. Continue in this way until all the edges of the centre patch are covered.

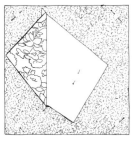

TRIMMING THE SQUARES
Work outwards until the square is complete. Make sure that there are no gaps or raw edges. When all the squares are finished, use the smaller template to mark and trim each square. Stitching at joining stage will prevent loose ends from unravelling.

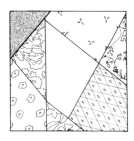

JOINING BLOCKS TOGETHER

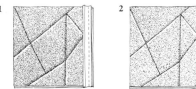 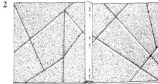

1   2

SETTING ROWS TOGETHER

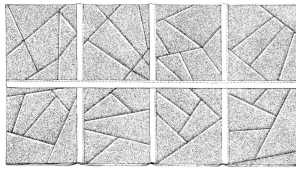

JOINING BLOCKS TOGETHER
1 *Cut a strip of tape to the length of one side of the patchwork squares. Put two squares right sides together and position the tape on top, matching the edge of the tape with the edges of the squares. Pin the tape in position, then sew through all the layers.*

2 *Open the work out flat, wrong side up, and bring the tape over to cover the seam.*

Pin the tape and sew it in position by hand, using a small running stitch and passing it through the backing only. Repeat until the units have been sewn into rows.

SETTING ROWS TOGETHER
Cut tape, this time to fit the row. Pin two rows, right sides together, with the tape on top. Sew through all layers, then open the work out flat and stitch the tape down by hand.

ITALIAN AND TRAPUNTO QUILTING

These are two attractive quilting techniques which were developed for their decorative effect rather than for warmth. In Italian (or cord) quilting, narrow channels are stitched and special quilting wool is pulled through them to raise the surface. In trapunto (stuffed) quilting, the design outlines are stitched and kapok or a synthetic wadding is then inserted. The strong lines of Italian quilting can be emphasized with machine stitching, but both techniques are suitable for hand or machine sewing and are worked from the back, using two layers of fabric. If you are sewing small blocks or units, rather than a full-size quilt, it is advisable to use a hoop.

Traditionally, plain fabrics were used, but more interesting effects can be obtained with striped fabrics or by using a transparent top and coloured wool (this technique is known as shadow quilting). For more details about fabrics and equipment, see p161.

ITALIAN QUILTING

This is suited to linear designs formed by intersecting or maze-like channels. If your pattern combines Italian quilting with trapunto, work the Italian areas first. The channels will vary in width according to the thickness of the wool used, but if they are to be filled with quilting wool the lines of stitching should be spaced 6mm ($\frac{1}{4}$in) apart. The work tends to shrink with quilting, so allow for this at the planning stage.

PREPARING TO SEW

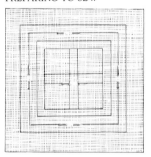

STITCHING THE PATTERN

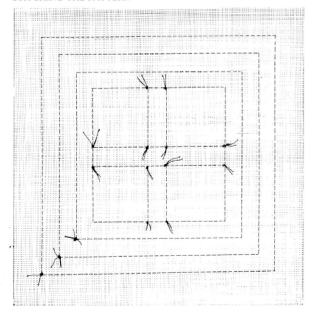

PREPARING TO SEW
Cut the top and backing fabrics to the same size, allowing for shrinkage and trimming. Mark the design on the right side of the backing fabric, spacing the lines 6mm ($\frac{1}{4}$in) to make channels through which the wool can be inserted. Use the tracing method (see p164) to mark the design, then pin the top and backing fabrics wrong sides together. Pin along the marked lines to avoid pin holes which might show on the finished work. For larger areas, tack rather than pin.

STITCHING THE PATTERN
Stitch along the marked lines, choosing a sewing sequence that does not entail continual stopping and starting. Stitch the main outlines of the pattern first, then any secondary lines, and finally the more intricate details. For hand sewing, use a running stitch or, preferably, a back stitch, which produces a solid stitching line. For machine sewing, set the machine to 3–4 stitches per centimetre (8–10 per inch). Pull the ends through to the back, tie the pairs together and trim them.

STRAIGHT CHANNELS

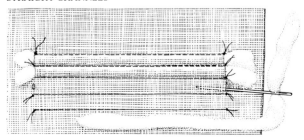

If the lines of quilting are very close, the rows can be finished with back stitching, as this will be concealed by the padding.

STRAIGHT CHANNELS
Thread a bodkin with quilting wool and gently ease apart the threads of the backing fabric at the start of a line. Insert the bodkin along the channel and pull the wool gently through so that it comfortably fills the space. Bring the bodkin out at the other end, again easing apart the threads of the backing fabric. Trim the wool, leaving about 1cm ($\frac{3}{8}$in) spare at either end. Always make sure before starting that you have enough wool to complete the line, and take care not to push the bodkin through the top fabric.

TURNING CORNERS

To avoid puckering the fabric at the corners, bring the bodkin out at the back when you reach a corner, then reinsert it at the same point, leaving a small loop of wool.

CROSSING LINES

If lines of quilting cross at any point in the design, make only one pair of stitched lines (one channel) continuous. The other channel should run right up to the line at either side of the first channel, but should not cross it. Start by inserting the wool into the continuous channel, then make the second channel, bringing the bodkin out at the intersection and reinserting it at the other side. If you are working on a large design, stitch all the continuous channels first.

TURNING CORNERS back

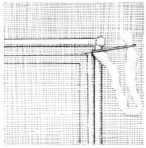

front

CROSSING LINES back

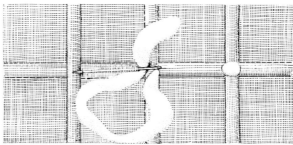

front

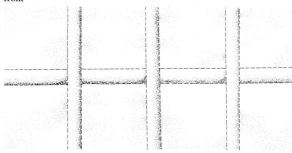

TRAPUNTO

In the past, trapunto was a hand sewing technique used to make complex and delicate relief designs, often with a floral theme, but it combines very well with Italian quilting in more modern geometric patterns, which are generally most effective when machine sewn. The method of inserting the filling can also be used for *broderie perse* and other types of appliqué.

FINISHING back

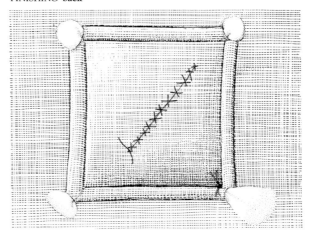

front

INSERTING THE STUFFING

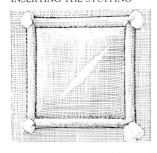

INSERTING THE STUFFING

Mark the backing fabric in the same way as described for Italian quilting, and stitch the outlines, then use a small crochet hook to insert the stuffing and pad out the shapes. When working on small areas, simply ease the threads of the backing fabric apart, making a small hole through which the stuffing can

be pushed. On larger areas it is necessary to cut a small slit. Gently and evenly fill the shape, starting with any corners. Insert stuffing a little at a time, using just enough to create a relief effect: too much filling can distort the shape, especially of smaller pieces.

FINISHING

When outlines have been filled, the holes are then closed with small overcast stitches. This applies to holes made with a hook as well as to slits, though in the case of small holes it is sometimes possible to ease the threads back into position with the hook or the point of a needle. When the work is complete, add a separate backing to protect and neaten the work.

FINISHING THE WORK

The last stage of quiltmaking is to finish the edges, the exception being quilts in which the layers are held together by buttons or tufts, as these are added after the edges are completed.

COMPLETING THE EDGES

There are several ways to close the edges. If you are bringing the backing over to the front to make a self binding, make sure that you have enough backing fabric and wadding to fill the border. Another method is to fold the edges of the top and backing inwards and hold them together with a running stitch (hand stitching is slower than machining but it often proves more manageable and it also looks better if the rest of the top is hand quilted). Or add a separate binding.

FOLDED EDGES

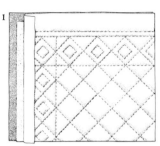

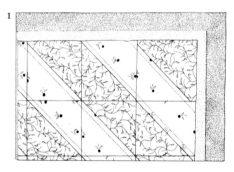

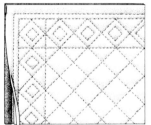

SELF BINDING

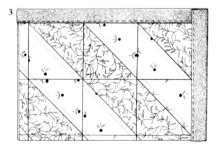
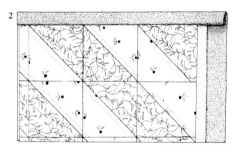

SELF BINDING
It is important to decide at an early stage if a quilt is to be self bound, so that additional materials are allowed for and a backing fabric is chosen which looks good when brought over to the front.

1 First neaten the edges of the top fabric, backing and wadding, if this is necessary. Allow enough backing fabric, including a 6mm (¼in) seam allowance, to give the required width of border. Trim the wadding to come up to the finished edge of the border. Do not trim it right back to the size of the top.

2 Fold over the seam allowance all round the edges of the backing and bring the fabric over to the top. Fold and pin the top and bottom edges of the quilt first, then the sides, making straight folds or mitres at the corners (see p156).

3 Secure the edges with a small hand running stitch or by machine. If you are machine stitching, make sure that the fabric lies evenly and does not gather at one end.

FOLDED EDGES
This method does not require any additional fabric and is the simplest way to close the edges, but the quilting pattern must stop about 1.5cm (⅝in) in from the edge so that the backing fabric is free to be folded over the wadding.

1 Trim the top and backing to neaten them. Trim the wadding, bearing in mind that it should extend about 1.5cm beyond the quilting lines. The top and backing should extend 1cm (⅜in) beyond the edge of the wadding.

2 Fold the backing fabric evenly over the wadding and pin, working clockwise and turning over one edge at a time. Turn under the edge of the top fabric and align it with the folded back edge down one side, pinning the two together. Repeat for each side.

3 Stitch the folded edges together by hand with small running stitches, making sure that you also secure the wadding. If desired, a second row of stitches can be made close to the first.

BOUND EDGES

Bindings can be purchased or you can make a binding from one of the fabrics used in the quilt, cutting strips on the bias if the corners are rounded.

1 *Trim the top, wadding and backing to the same size, leaving a 6mm (¼in) seam allowance.*

2 *Fold over one end of the binding, then, with right sides together and aligning raw edges, pin the binding to the top of the quilt, easing it round the corners. Machine stitch it in position.*

3 *Fold the binding over to the back of the quilt and sew it in place by hand with a running or overcast stitch, taking the needle through the backing fabric only.*

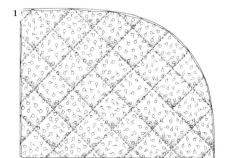
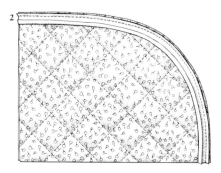
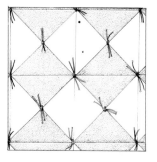
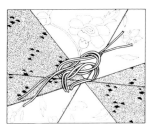

BUTTONING AND TUFTING

If you do not want to quilt a top (or for that matter if you just want to prevent the two layers of a coverlet from slipping), buttoning or tufting, which is also known as tying, are two quick and easy ways of keeping the layers together. Buttons or tufts are added after the edges of the quilt have been closed. They can be positioned either as an additional form of decoration or in line with the basic grid or pattern. If they are to hold the layers securely, they should ideally be spaced from 10 to 15cm (4 to 6in) apart, and in patchwork quilts they are often placed on a seam line. Buttons can be stitched in pairs, one on either side, or just on one side of the quilt. Whether you are using buttons or tufts, make sure that the stitches are not too tight, particularly if the fabrics used in the quilt are relatively fine, as this might eventually lead to tearing.

BUTTONING

Either flat or shank buttons can be used. Start by pinning or tacking the layers together, making sure that the area on either side of the button position lies flat. Use a double thickness of button thread and pull the needle through from the top, losing the ends in between the layers. Make a small cross stitch before attaching the button and sew through all layers.

If you are decorating the back of the work as well as the front by using two buttons, attach both buttons at once. Finish by again losing the ends of thread between the layers.

Embroidery or other beads can be used as an alternative

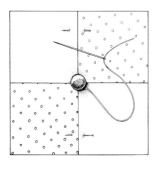
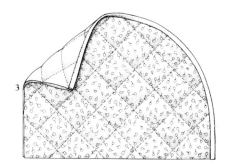

to buttons, perhaps with beads of varying colours arranged in a pattern to complement the fabrics and design of the patchwork. There must, however, be enough beads or buttons to serve the practical purpose of holding the layers together.

TUFTING

Use a chenille needle, which is sharp but can take thick thread, and an all-cotton thread, such as crochet cotton, which will hold the knot. (Do not use wool because it felts.) Thread the needle with a double thickness and, starting from the top, sew through all the layers, leaving an end about 3cm (1¼in) long on top. Bring the needle up, then bring it down and back through the first hole again. Bring it back up to the top and trim the thread to the same length as the other end.

Tie the two ends together, using a reef knot, as shown here (right over left, left over right). Trim the ends to the desired length.

BLOCK PATTERNS

The essential thing about all block patterns is that they are based on a grid, which is nearly always divided into squares of equal size and traditionally the number of squares in a block defines the category into which the block falls. The chief categories are listed below and some examples are shown on the following pages.

ENLARGING OR REDUCING DESIGNS

If you wish to copy a patchwork block or to use a picture as the basis of an appliqué design, it is often necessary to scale up the image to the required size, either using a photocopying process, or by drawing up a grid, as shown.

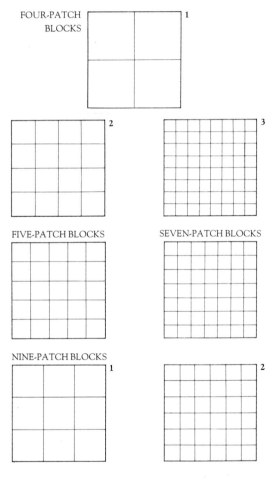

FOUR-PATCH BLOCKS

FIVE-PATCH BLOCKS   SEVEN-PATCH BLOCKS

NINE-PATCH BLOCKS

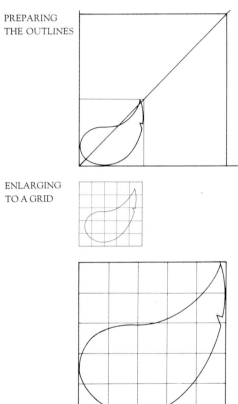

PREPARING THE OUTLINES

ENLARGING TO A GRID

FOUR-PATCH BLOCKS
Four-patch grids are those with 4, 16 or 64 squares altogether (2, 4 or 8 across).

FIVE-PATCH BLOCKS
These generally have 5 squares across or 25 squares, though they can have 10 squares across, making 100 altogether.

SEVEN-PATCH BLOCKS
These have 7 squares across, or 49 squares in total.

NINE-PATCH BLOCKS
The traditional name for this category is somewhat misleading, as it embraces blocks that have 36 squares altogether (6 across) as well as simpler grids with 3 squares each way (9 in total).

PREPARING THE OUTLINES
Blocks are easy to scale up because they are designed to fit a grid, but for other images you must first trace off the design and then enclose it in a square or rectangle. Cut this out and tape it in one corner of a larger sheet of paper. Draw the baseline out to the desired width of the larger image, then draw a vertical line. Draw a diagonal from one corner of the tracing to the other, as shown, and continue it to meet the vertical line. This will give you the correct proportions.

ENLARGING TO A GRID
Next, remove the tracing and draw a grid on it composed of small, equal-sized squares. Draw a grid of exactly the same number of squares on the larger outline, then copy the image freehand, square by square. If you are copying a block, all you need do is to work out the grid for the block and draw this up to the larger size: the patches will all be shaped to fit the grid squares. The blocks shown on the following pages can be used in this way.

A SELECTION OF TRADITIONAL PATTERNS

FOUR-PATCH

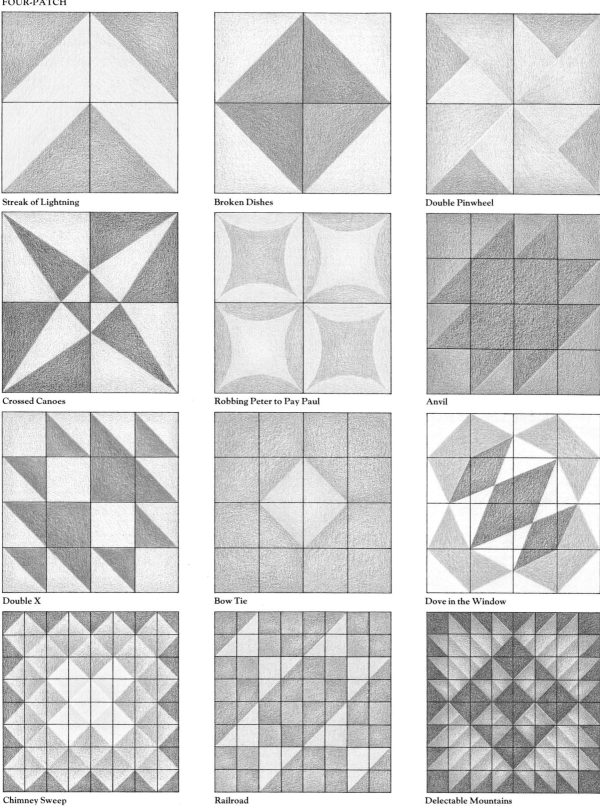

Streak of Lightning

Broken Dishes

Double Pinwheel

Crossed Canoes

Robbing Peter to Pay Paul

Anvil

Double X

Bow Tie

Dove in the Window

Chimney Sweep

Railroad

Delectable Mountains

FIVE-PATCH

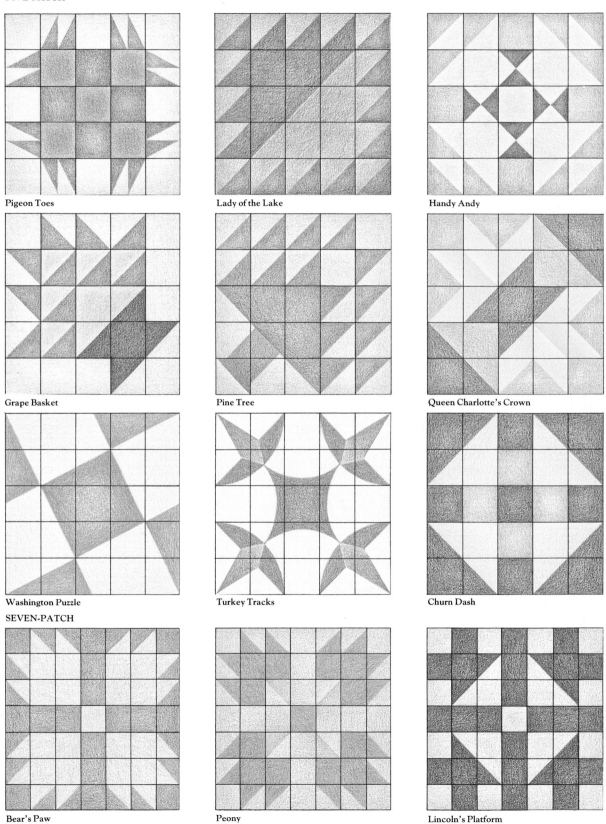

Pigeon Toes

Lady of the Lake

Handy Andy

Grape Basket

Pine Tree

Queen Charlotte's Crown

Washington Puzzle

Turkey Tracks

Churn Dash

SEVEN-PATCH

Bear's Paw

Peony

Lincoln's Platform

NINE-PATCH

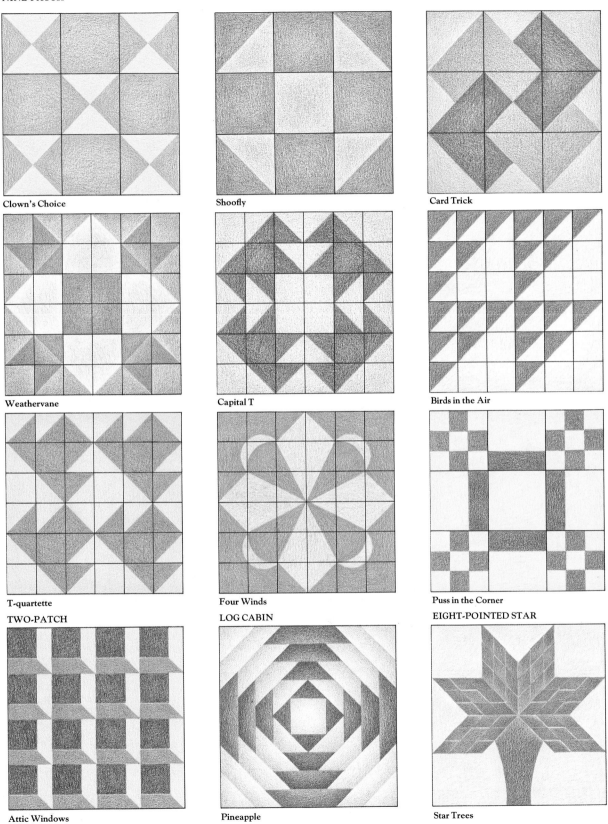

Clown's Choice

Shoofly

Card Trick

Weathervane

Capital T

Birds in the Air

T-quartette

Four Winds

Puss in the Corner

TWO-PATCH

LOG CABIN

EIGHT-POINTED STAR

Attic Windows

Pineapple

Star Trees

PATCHWORK TEMPLATES

Isosceles triangle

Square

Right-angled triangle

Parallelogram

Trapezoid

Rectangle

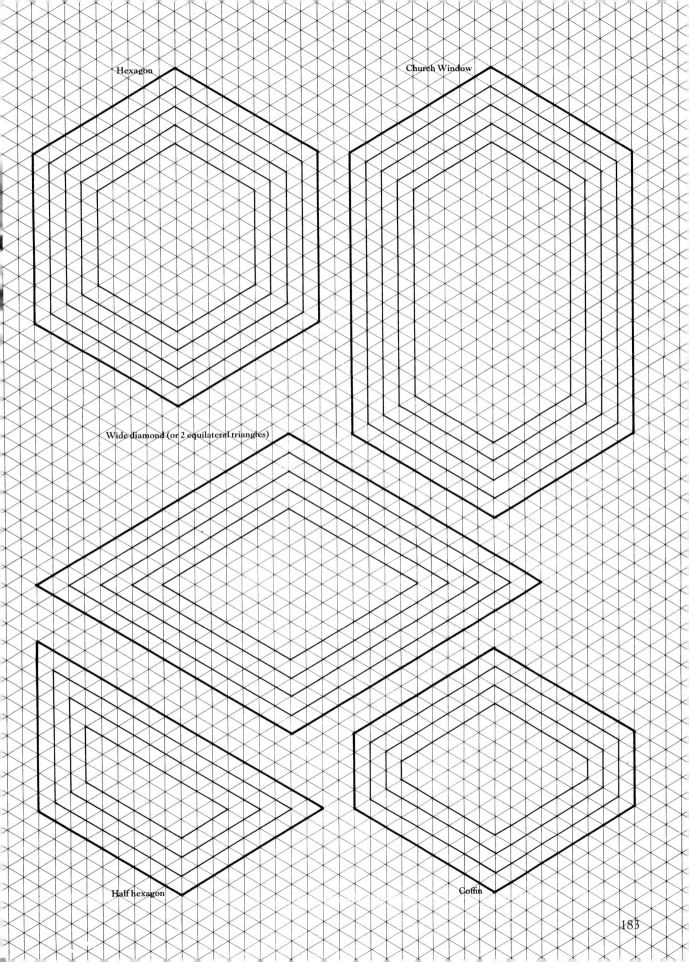

Hexagon

Church Window

Wide diamond (or 2 equilateral triangles)

Half hexagon

Coffin

183

QUILTING TEMPLATES

Scissors (mirror image to make a pair)

Rose

Tear (feather shape)

Curved feather

Lined twist

Shell

Flower

CARING FOR QUILTS

Quite apart from any subjective value a quilt may have – as a part of family history or because you yourself put a great deal of care and effort into making it – quilts over about 50 years old have a considerable intrinsic value. If your quilt falls into this category and is fragile or delicate, it would be worth leaving any cleaning or repair work to a textile expert. You would not, after all, dream of attempting to clean a valuable oil painting yourself, and an antique quilt is equally deserving of professional attention. With this proviso, the following tips and hints are intended to give general guidance on caring for your quilts.

CLEANING

One way of cleaning a quilt without risking a wet wash is to vacuum it to remove surface dust and dirt particles. Lay the quilt out flat and cover it with a thin muslin or similar fabric to protect it from direct suction. Old mosquito netting, if you happen to have it, is ideal for this purpose. Otherwise, use a cheap, fine muslin, or even net curtains.

Vacuum cleaning is useful for quilts that can be neither washed nor dry-cleaned and it is also a sensible preliminary exercise to remove loose dirt before washing.

Testing for dye-fastness

Before washing a quilt, always test it for dye-fastness, bearing in mind that while some patches may be dye-fast, others may run. There is no strict rule, but in general strong, dark colours, especially indigo blue, are more likely to run than light ones.

Start by putting a few drops of water on the area to be tested and then use white blotting paper to soak it up. If no stain appears, repeat the test with a solution of detergent and water. Remember that the fabrics used in a patchwork or appliqué quilt may have come from a wide range of sources,

so do not assume that the quilt can be washed on the basis of just one tested patch.

Washing

In addition to testing for dye-fastness, it is also necessary to determine the composition of the fabrics used in a quilt before you risk washing them. Normally, wool and silk should be dry-cleaned, while cotton and linen may be washed; some fillings can also cause problems.

If your quilt can be washed safely, the bath tub is generally the best place to do it. This, however, may not be large enough for a big quilt, and cramming a large wet quilt into a confined space can cause tearing. Use a mild detergent – soaps can cause yellowing – and avoid heavy duty detergents, especially biological washing powders. Make sure that the detergent is fully dissolved before you immerse the quilt in the water, which should be warm, not hot.

If you are washing the quilt in a bath tub, fold it in such a way that the corners are easily accessible since this makes handling easier. Agitate the quilt gently to ease out the dirt. If it is heavily soiled, it is best to give it several gentle washes.

Quilts become heavy when wet and can easily tear, so let the water drain out of the bath and refill the tub without attempting to lift the quilt. Rinse as many times as you need to get rid of all traces of the detergent. Use a shower attachment if you have one. After the final rinse, gently press as much water as possible out of the quilt before lifting it.

Great care is needed at this stage to avoid tearing the quilt or breaking the stitches. If you can, get someone to help you and try to distribute the weight as evenly as possible. Carefully lift the quilt out of the tub and place it on large, absorbent towels, then press out the excess moisture.

Drying

When you have removed as much excess moisture as possible, lay the quilt out to dry. On bright dry days, this can be done outside, providing you keep it out of direct sunlight. Spread a clean sheet on the ground, lay the quilt flat on it, then gently ease it into shape.

If the quilt must be dried indoors, lay it flat and then gently roll it up with dry towels, repeating the process until you have removed as much moisture as possible.

Never hang a quilt on a washing line or clothes horse, since this method, although traditional, does not distribute the weight evenly enough for safety.

REPAIRS

Like washing, the question of whether to repair a quilt yourself or to seek professional advice and help depends on the value you set on the quilt itself, the condition of the fabrics, and your own skill. There is not in itself anything wrong in repairing a quilt – mending tears, replacing a worn edging strip or using the skills of an expert needlewoman to reweave a lost area of fabric. Such repairs are part of the normal life of a quilt and can help to strengthen it. There is a great deal of truth in the old saying that a stitch in time saves nine.

It is, however, important that any repairs should be in sympathy with the nature of the quilt. On a hand-sewn quilt, for example, all repairs should be worked by hand, including the replacement of a worn edge (keep the old binding as a record). If some fabrics are so worn that there is nothing left, it may be best to leave the quilt alone: most modern fabrics will look incongruous within the context of an old quilt, and fabrics that resemble the originals may be hard to find. You might, however, try dipping fabrics in cold tea which at least helps to reduce the harshness and brightness of modern dyes.

STORAGE

Correct storage is an important part of quilt conservation. One of the easiest and best

Repeating blocks of three strips of lightweight wool, in pieced lattice strips of heavy grey cotton. Canadian. Late 19th century. 163 × 142cm (64 × 56in).

ways to store a quilt is to put it to its original use by laying it flat on a bed. If this is impractical it can either be carefully rolled over a large cardboard tube or folded. If you are using a cardboard tube (a method which is best suited to coverlets or quilts that are not densely quilted), you should first wrap the tube with a protective layer of acid-free tissue paper, then gently roll the quilt on to the tube and finish by wrapping it in clean cotton sheeting.

A quilt that has been folded for storage can suffer permanent creasing and at worst it may be seriously damaged where the fabric has become worn on the folds. Ideally, therefore, the quilt should be refolded every two months or so. Unfortunately, the very process of folding can damage a very fragile quilt, which should be handled as little as possible. If you do have to fold a quilt for storage, fold it in thirds and pad all folds with acid-free tissue paper and use the same paper to line wooden drawers or shelves.

Dust and grime can also damage fibres, so it is important to keep your quilt clean. Shake it regularly, taking care to be as gentle as possible, and use a hand vacuum cleaner, as already described. Finally make sure that your storage space is free from damp, and never store a quilt in a plastic bag, since textiles need to breathe to avoid rotting.

Southernwood (*Artemisia abrotanum*), an aromatic shrub, is an effective traditional method of fending off moths and other insects. Hang a bunch of it in your storage area to keep them at bay.

HANGING A QUILT

If you are displaying a quilt, or for that matter storing it on a bed, keep it away from direct sunlight, which can fade and weaken the fabrics, and be equally wary of spotlights and other strong domestic light sources.

Only quilts that are in good condition and not too heavy should be hung. There are two main ways of hanging a quilt. The first is to make a fabric sleeve about 10 to 15cm (4 to 6in) deep and sew it to the top of the quilt on the reverse side. The stitching should not go through the quilt top and the sleeve should stop short of the side edges of the quilt. A rod can then be threaded through the sleeve and secured to the wall. It may help to attach small eyelet hooks to each end of the rod, and if the rod itself is wooden then it should first be sealed with a polyurethane varnish, or a similar sealant, to prevent seepages from the wood staining the fabric. If the quilt is particularly wide and heavy it may be preferable to make the sleeve in two sections, leaving a gap in the middle to allow a centre fixing.

An alternative method is to use Velcro tape 5cm (2in) wide. One side of the Velcro is machine stitched to a strip of cotton tape 7.5cm (3in) wide, which is then hand-sewn to the reverse of the quilt. Use a combination of backstitch and herringbone stitch and, as with a sleeve, stitch through the backing and filling but not the quilt top, and stop short of the side edges. The other side of the Velcro is then stuck to a length of board, which must be sealed to prevent seepage.

Whether you use a rod inserted through sleeves or a board, the wooden mounting should be slightly shorter than the width of the quilt, so that it is not visible from the front. If you are using Velcro, check that it is adhering along the full length of the strip.

USEFUL ADDRESSES

Craft Publications
Unit 5c
5 West Hill
Aspley Guise
Milton Keynes MK17 8DP
Specialist needlework and craft magazines, as well as American books not published in Britain – mail order only

The Patchwork Dog and Calico Cat
21 Chalk Farm Road
London NW1
Fabrics, sewing and quilting equipment, books, and traditional quilts – available from the shop and by mail order

Quilters' Guild
Margaret Petit (secretary)
56 Wilcot Road
Pewsey
Wiltshire SNP 5EL
The guild publishes a quarterly magazine and organizes meetings and exhibitions – a good way of meeting fellow quilters

Strawberry Fayre Fabrics
Chagford
Devon TQ13 8EN
Fabrics and equipment – mail order only

Village Fabrics
30 Goldsmith's Lane
Wallingford
Oxfordshire OX10 0DN
An extensive range of fabrics – available from the shop and by mail order

QUILTING GROUPS

Western Australia Quilting Association
PO Box 55
Subiaco
Western Australia 6008

South African Quilting Association
Mrs B. Malan
41 Tennyson Road
Lombardy East,
Transvaal 2192
South Africa

INDEX

BIBLIOGRAPHY

Betterton, Shiela
Quilts and Coverlets from the American Museum in Britain
The American Museum in Britain, Bath, 1978

Beyer, Jinny
Patchwork Patterns
EPM Publications Inc, 1979; Bell & Hyman, 1982

Burbidge, Pauline
Making Patchwork for Pleasure and Profit
John Gifford, 1981

Dover Publications, New York
(A series of books on geometric design suitable for patchwork.)

Holstein, Jonathan
The Pieced Quilt
Galahad Books, 1973

Itten, Johannes
The Elements of Color
Van Nostrand Reinhold, 1970

James, Michael
The Quilter's Handbook; The Second Quilter's Handbook
Prentice Hall, 1978; 1981

Kiracofe and Kile
The Quilt Digest volumes 1, 2, 3
San Francisco, 1983, 1984, 1985

Pottinger, David
Quilts from the Indiana Amish
E.P. Dutton, 1983

Wade, David
Geometric Patterns and Borders
Wildwood House, 1982
Pattern in Islamic Art
Studio Vista, 1976

Wong, Wucius
Principles of Two-Dimensional Design
Van Nostrand Reinhold, 1968

AUTHOR'S ACKNOWLEDGMENTS

I would like to thank all the quiltmakers and collectors who have helped me in the preparation of this book. In particular, thanks to Ron Simpson, Paul Taylor, Jane Kasmin and Joen Zinni Lask for allowing me to borrow so many quilts from their private collections. I am very grateful to the British quiltmakers whose work I have photographed and recorded, and to the American designers, especially Michael James, who have contributed photographs of their quilts for the project. Thanks are due to Dinah Prentice and Deirdre Amsden for preparing work especially for the design chapter, and to Shiela Betterton for her help in authenticating the traditional quilts.

I owe a great debt to the team at Frances Lincoln for their hard work and enthusiasm in putting the book together, and to Paul Fletcher and Tig Sutton for making the quilts and the step-by-step instructions look so attractive. Finally, I would like to give special thanks to Pauline Burbidge and Lucy Goffin for the continuing encouragement they have given me throughout the project.

PUBLISHERS' ACKNOWLEDGMENTS

The publishers would like to thank the following people for their help in putting this book together: Susan Berry for her indefatigable work in helping the book meet its deadlines; Alison Freegard, Jonathan Hilton, Joanna Jellinek, Sarah Mitchell and Barty Phillips for their editorial contribution; Anne Hardy for compiling the index, and Debbie MacKinnon for art direction.

Illustrators

Grahame Corbett   pp178–85
Sally Launder   pp98–111, 116
Tig Sutton   pp132–77

Photographers

All photographs by Paul Fletcher except for the following:
David Caras pp9, 64–5
Geoffrey Newcombe p127 (bottom right)
David Ridge pp10, 34–5, 96, 112–13, 114–15, 118, 119 (top left, centre right), 120, 121 (bottom left and bottom right), 122, 123 (top right and centre right), 126, 127 (top), 128, 131

Project Editor   Penny David

Art Editor   Caroline Hill

Text Editor   Diana Mansour

The author and publishers wish to thank the following people and institutions for permission to reproduce their quilts in this book:

The American Museum in Britain, Bath: p153. **Deirdre Amsden**: 'Colourwash Studies' © 1981–84, pp34–5; North Country Plain Quilt © Amy Emms, pp92–3. **Barry Beckett and Berenice Shachar**: pp90–91. **Pauline Burbidge**: 'Cubic Log Cabin' © 1982, p7; 'Pyramid in Disguise' © 1985, p60; 'Stripy Step' © 1984, pp61 and 143. **Susan Carr**: 'Summer Garden' © 1984, pp28–9; Log Cabin quilt © 1983, p103; 'Marriage Quilt' © 1983, p133. **Chester County Council**: Library Screen © Lucy Goffin 1984, p127. **Crafts Council**, London: 'Twilight' © Eng Tow, p88; 'La Mer' © Phyllis Ross, pp70 and 89. **Crane Gallery, London**: pp16–17, 30, 149. **Nancy Crow**: 'Interfacings 1' © 1983, p6. **Pamela Dempster**: 'Colourwash Study' (p34, bottom left) © Deirdre Amsden. **Lucy Goffin**: p49. **Diana Harris**: 'Three Squares' © 1982. **Iona Heath**: 'First and Last', p27; 'Tailor's Stars', p135; 'Reds under the Bed', p157. **Michael James**: 'Metamorphosis' © 1983, p9; 'La Tempete' © 1983, p64; 'Blue Undercurrents' © 1983, p65 and 105; 'The Sixth Exercise', 'Spanish Dance', p124–5. **Jane Kasmin**: pp10, 20–21, 22–3, 26, 36–7, 54, 68–9. **Krogstad Design Inc**: 'Contained Crazy' © Jan Myers 1984, pp56–7. **Joen Zinni Lask**: pp40, 48, 139. **Linda MacDonald**: 'Clean Getaway' © 1983, pp94–5, 'Shooting Gallery' © 1983, p107. **Dawn Pavitt**: 'Nine Fold Harmony', p167. **Dinah Prentice**: 'Molesworth Mon Amour' © 1983, pp84–5 and 123; 'Sienna Stones' and 'Hermeneutics', pp122–3. **Robert and Lisa Sainsbury Collection**: p87. **Ron Simpson and Paul Taylor**: pp14–15, 18–19, 24–5, 31, 32–3, 41, 42–3, 44–5, 46–7, 52–3, 55, 58–9, 62, 63, 66, 67, 72–3, 76–7, 78–9, 80–81, 82–3, 86 140, 155, 169, 187. **Michele Walker**: 'Colour Variations' © 1981–4, pp50–51 and 165. **Julie Zinni**: pp74–5 and 150.

Jacket photography

Star quilt   Paul Fletcher
Plain quilt   Ian O'Leary
Back flap   David Ridge

Colour separation by DS Colour International Ltd